1004941488

Document Delivery and Interlibrary Loan on a Shoestring

EMILY KNOX

Neal-Schuman Publishers, Inc.

New York   London

Published by Neal-Schuman Publishers, Inc.
100 William St., Suite 2004
New York, NY 10038

Printed and bound in the United States of America.

The paper used in this publication meets the minimum requirements of American National Standard for Information Sciences—Permanence of Paper for Printed Library Materials, ANSI Z39.48-1992.

Library of Congress Cataloging-in-Publication Data

Knox, Emily, 1976-
   Document delivery and interlibrary loan on a shoestring / Emily Knox.
     p. cm.
   Includes bibliographical references and index.
   ISBN 978-1-55570-678-4 (alk. paper)
    1. Interlibrary loans—United States. 2. Document delivery—United States.
3. Small libraries—Circulation and loans—United States. I. Title.

Z713.5.U6K62 2010
025.6'20973—dc22

2009035189

Table of Contents

List of Figures

Preface

Interlibrary loan (ILL) and document delivery services are critical to today's library service. They allow libraries to provide information at the time of need instead of buying or subscribing to materials in case they will one day be needed. In addition to supplying users with information quickly, they also facilitate networking with other libraries.

However, processing interlibrary loan and document delivery requests takes time. Handling the many lending and borrowing requests that a library receives each week can eat into the workday. If you are an interlibrary loan librarian in a larger library, this is not a problem—ILL is part of your primary job responsibility. However, if you are a librarian or information professional in a medium- to small-sized library, interlibrary loan and document delivery may be just one task on a long list of responsibilities. Reference and circulation librarians are often called upon to provide ILL services to patrons even though they have little training or support in this job function. Smaller institutions with low numbers of requests may not wish to assign a large amount of staff time to interlibrary loan functions and may find it difficult to justify the purchase of time-saving technology for a tiny ILL operation.

Document Delivery and Interlibrary Loan on a Shoestring was written for librarians newly assigned to interlibrary loan and document delivery responsibilities as well as interlibrary loan librarians in smaller libraries, although the book also provides information and tips that would be useful in all libraries. This manual also describes general best practices modified for the one-person ILL service. It is written for both the information professional just starting in a position that includes ILL duties and for the established staff person who would like to make his or her operation more efficient. This manual introduces ILL policies and procedures, provides time-saving hints and tips, and suggests how to get the most from affordable technologies that support these services.

Chapter 1 presents working definitions of interlibrary loan and document delivery as well as a brief introduction to the history of interlibrary loan and its place in library services. It also provides guidelines for modifying existing best practices to suit a smaller institution's needs. Chapter 2 looks at the issues that are prevalent in small interlibrary loan and document delivery departments and provides ways for dealing with them. Chapter 3 discusses copyright law and regulations; it is critical that all librarians be familiar with and adhere to the law. Chapter 4 covers the various national, state, and local codes that guide interlibrary loan with special emphasis on the National Interlibrary Loan Code for the United States developed by the Reference and User Services Association of the American Library Association.

Developing a good policy is one of the most important aspects of providing efficient and cost-effective interlibrary loan and document delivery service. Policies in very small library departments should be developed with an eye toward saving the time of both the patron and the staff members, while preserving high standards of customer service. Chapter 5 offers suggestions for crafting good interlibrary loan policy. Chapters 6 and 7 provide many more specific suggestions for lending and borrowing policies and procedures.

Chapter 8 presents traditional technology solutions for interlibrary loan and document delivery service. All staff members who handle ILL services should be familiar with these systems since information about them appears in borrowing requests. The chapter discusses why these systems provide many benefits if a department can afford them, though they are not integral to providing small-scale interlibrary loan and document delivery service.

Chapter 9 illustrates how to provide interlibrary loan and document delivery services without paying for a comprehensive ILL management system or using commercial document delivery systems. It describes how to use widely available office technology and open source products to electronically receive and track ILL and document delivery transactions.

So that readers don't have to look for forms and the ILL code, figures throughout the book feature time-saving templates for ILL forms as well as policy examples, and Appendixes A and B include the text of the Interlibrary Loan Code for the United States.

Most ILL and document delivery manuals are written from the perspective of a large interlibrary loan service manager. The authors often assume that the reader has access to the latest technology. This manual assumes that readers do not have adequate staff, financial, or technology resources to allocate to interlibrary loan or commercial document delivery services. This does not mean that the services provided by the small ILL department are poor. They just require more technological ingenuity and time-management skills. This manual will give you the tools you need to get ILL and document delivery done.

Acknowledgments

Writing this manual has been an exhilarating (and sometimes painful) process and I would like to thank some of the many people who helped me along the way. My editor at Neal-Schuman, Sandy Wood, always kept me on track. Thanks go to Laura Moore, V. K. McCarty, R. Bruce Mullin, and everyone at the General Theological Seminary who encouraged me throughout the proposal process. Marie Radford at the School of Communication and Information at Rutgers University gave me excellent time management advice that I should have followed more carefully. My friends Simon Lawrence, Kyle Peppers, Anika Penn, Nancy Friedrich, and Genesis Fisher always had a sympathetic ear. Lauren Siebert and I had a few late-night conversations about interlibrary loan and librarianship. My brother, Gordon Knox, helped me with some of the legal issues. Special thanks go to Leon Laureij, who kept me going through some of the more difficult moments of the writing process. Finally, I would like to thank my parents, Nathaniel and Jo Emily Knox, who have always given me their love and support.

Essentials of Interlibrary Loan and Document Delivery

Interlibrary loan is at the heart of the library's objective to provide information to patrons because it helps fulfill the library's mission to provide patrons' with whatever they need, even if the library does not own the material. Interlibrary loan beautifully exemplifies S.R. Ranganathan's second and third Laws of Library Science: "Every Reader His or Her Book" and "Every Book Its Reader." It allows readers to find their books even if they are geographically distant from one another.

Interlibrary loan also pushes libraries and librarians to cooperate with other members of the wider library and information community. For small libraries, borrowing books and sending articles all over the country provides an entrance into the larger world of library networks. In an ideal world, when libraries provide these services it means that any book or article, anywhere in the world, is available to patrons no matter where they are located.

Unfortunately, many of these services are constrained by budgets, staff limitations, and legal restrictions. In many libraries interlibrary loan is simply an afterthought—the last item in a long list of duties for the reference librarian or public services assistant. Some libraries continue to employ outdated or inefficient policies and procedures even after changes in technology make them obsolete. Because they conduct only a few transactions per year and the policies do not inhibit patrons' ability to get the materials they need for research, many libraries do not revise interlibrary loan policies on a regular basis. Even within these boundaries, however, any library or information center can provide excellent inter-library loan and document delivery service. Such a service fulfills Ranganathan's fourth Law: Save the Time of the Reader (Ranganathan, 1957). This efficiency can also save the time of the library staff.

One of the major problems with interlibrary loan is its invisibility. From the patron's point of view, interlibrary loan is simply magic. The patron requires a book or article that is not owned by the local library. She or he puts in a request, often by pressing a button, sometimes by filling out a form. A few days or weeks later, the item appears in the local library or in the patron's e-mail inbox. The entire transaction did not require any interaction between the user and the library staff. The patron never sees all of the time-consuming steps involved in the process: printing out the request, walking through the stacks to find the book, placing it in an envelope with the correct mailing address, then dropping it in the mail, picking up the mail, processing the item, and then sending it to the hold shelf. He or she asked for an item located halfway across the country and, like magic, it appeared on the doorstep.

This chapter provides a brief background to interlibrary loan services. It begins with some definitions of common terms. It then provides a brief history of interlibrary loan and document delivery. Next, the chapter describes the reasoning behind specialist-developed best practices for interlibrary loan. The chapter concludes with a description of my rationale for modifying best practices for small departments.

Defining Interlibrary Loan Terms

Interlibrary loan (ILL) is an umbrella term that encompasses all the services, policies, and procedures involved when libraries share materials (Hilyer, 2006). The most common definition is stated in the 2008 national *Interlibrary Loan Code for the United States* (reproduced in Appendix A), which defines ILL as "the process by which a library requests material from, or supplies material to, another library" (American Library Association, 2008a: Section 1.0). The explanatory guidelines for the code (reproduced in Appendix B) note that the purpose of interlibrary loan is to supplement local collections (American Library Association, 2008b).

Different organizations use different umbrella terms for this service, including resource sharing, document delivery, interlending, and interlibrary services. These terms differ in semantics with some focusing on the types of materials lent or the transmission channels that are used for sharing resources. Whichever term is used, the general steps needed for completing a transaction remain the same.

The term "document delivery" deserves a bit more explanation. In the late twentieth century, document delivery specifically referred to obtaining materials, particularly articles, from a fee-based service (Boucher, 1997). Over the past decade, computer technology such as full-text databases have become ubiquitous, and this term has lost much of its specificity. In library service, the work should be primary, not the form in which it is accessed, and this term excessively focuses on the form and delivery method of the material requested. For the purposes of this manual, document delivery is simply another aspect of ILL. It should be noted, however, that many libraries maintain the distinction and refer to their resource-sharing service as "Interlibrary Loan and Document Delivery."

Two institutions are involved in an interlibrary loan transaction: the requesting library that asks for the material and the supplying library that fulfills the request. The requesting library is the borrower and the supplying library is the lender.

ILL refers to two different procedures: interlibrary lending and interlibrary borrowing. These procedures are completely distinct from each other. They require different forms and processes and, in large institutions, are sometimes handled by different staff members.

Different countries employ different types of ILL service. In an article discussing ILL protocols, Mary Jackson specifies two models for interlibrary loan: library mediated and patron mediated (Jackson, 1997). There are four types of library-mediated service. The United Kingdom uses a centralized service through British Library Lending Division. Another type of ILL service, such as the one in German, is hierarchical and uses a tired request system (Jackson, 1997). This book focuses on the decentralized system used in the United States in which each institution creates its own policies and handles its own transactions. The fourth type of library mediated ILL is a mixed model employing a combination of the other three models.

For the purposes of this manual, a small interlibrary loan department is defined as one that conducts 500 or fewer borrowing and lending transactions per year. Staff members of departments that process more transactions might be interested in the time-saving suggestions given throughout the book. However, the manual focuses on departments that cannot afford (and do not necessarily need) an interlibrary loan management system.

History of Interlibrary Loan

Development of Codes

Although no precise date is recorded for the beginning of interlibrary loan, it is evident that by the time Melvil Dewey first organized the American Library Association (ALA) in 1876, informal networks for interlibrary borrowing already existed. The first issue of the *American Library Journal* (now called *Library Journal*), the professional journal of ALA, includes a letter from Samuel S. Green, librarian of Worcester Free Public Library, that plainly discusses his concerns regarding interlibrary lending.

Green's letter, dated September 4, 1876, provides some insight into the need for interlibrary loan in the late nineteenth century and also shows that the service has not changed much since then. Green states that "it would add greatly to the usefulness of our reference libraries if an agreement should be made to lend books to each other for short periods of time" (Green, 1876: 15). He notes that "not unfrequently" patrons ask for a book that the library does not own but would take too much time to buy.

According to Green, the Boston Public Library allows nonresidents to take out books, but perhaps libraries would prefer to send books to other libraries rather than to individuals where they would be "looked after as they look after their own books" (Green, 1876: 15). This is one of the innovations of interlibrary loan: responsibility for the items rests with the borrowing library rather than the individual requesting the book. Green then states that he believes that libraries would be willing to not only accept responsibility for the borrowed books but also pay for shipment. Apparently, "a plan of this kind is in operation in Europe" (Green, 1876: 16).

Green ends by commenting that the library in Worcester might not be able to participate in such a plan but that should not keep other libraries from developing one. He also suggests that the librarians discuss the matter at the upcoming conference in Philadelphia. Although Mr. Green was present at the first American Library Association conference later that year, the sessions did not include any discussion of cooperative borrowing and lending between libraries. In fact, it was not on the conference agenda until 1899.

Interlibrary loan continued within informal networks of libraries throughout the late nineteenth and early twentieth centuries, but it was not until 1916 that the first interlibrary loan code was published. Adopted by ALA in 1919, it was noteworthy for being almost universally ignored by librarians. A cursory glance at the code sheds some light on the reason for being ignored: current fiction, which is described as a book "requested for a trivial purpose," could not be shared. Also, the code required that the borrowing library pay all expenses and borrowed books had to be used inside the library. Finally, only those deemed serious scholars had the privilege of ILL service. This excluded undergraduate students as well as graduate students.

The second national ILL code, adopted in 1940 by ALA, was even narrower than the previous one and was also widely ignored by librarians. According to a survey completed in 1952, librarians questioned the need for borrowing libraries to bear all expenses and whether it was appropriate to exclude "unserious" materials.

An article from *College and Research Libraries* from October 1952 neatly sums up the problems with the 1952 code in its title "Interlibrary Loan—Smothered in Tradition." The writer, Walter W. Wright of the University of Pennsylvania Library, laments that libraries are "following traditional costly procedures" including chariness in lending rare books, duplicating records, expensive shipping methods, and the overly restrictive building-use-only provision. Wright's comments on collecting shipping postage deserve a longer quote:

> . . . carriage costs constitute but a small part of interlibrary loan costs, emphasized probably because they are easily measured and represent out-of-pocket expense. We have received postal cards stating that we owed small amounts like 13 or 16 cents. We were sorry that we failed to return this postage but it was hard to avoid the conclusion that our colleague libraries had spent much more than the amounts claimed collecting them. (Wright, 1952: 332)

The 1940 code lasted only 12 years.

It is clear from both Green's letter and Wright's article that the issues surrounding interlibrary loan changed little over 75 years. The problems they describe are familiar to anyone who has worked in interlibrary loan services. In order to ameliorate the problems discussed by Wright in 1952, ALA issued another code in 1968. This one did allow graduate students to use ILL but, once again, neither the 1952 code nor the 1968 code was universally accepted by the library community.

Two years after the adoption of the 1968 code, the American Library Association published the first *Interlibrary Loan Procedure Manual*. It provided an annotation of the 1968 code along with forms and instructions for sharing materials. However, the scope for lending and borrowing items was still restricted to "research."

New codes were developed in 1980 and in 1993. Both of these codes recognized the large number of state and local codes that had developed throughout the country. The local codes had a profound effect on the national code and eventually led to its liberalization. The purpose and scope of the most recent national code, developed in 2008, is discussed more fully in Chapter 3.

National standards for the interlibrary loan form also developed along with the codes. The first national form, adopted by the Association of College and Research Libraries in 1951 was created by the University of California. Although used less frequently today, the ALA ILL form is accepted by almost all libraries across the country.

The history of interlibrary loan was greatly affected by three improvements in library service: the development of a national union catalog, the expansion of library networks, and advances in communication technology. The 1960s and 1970s experienced an explosion in interlibrary loan transactions and this growth is generally attributed to these three developments.

The Union Catalog

A true union catalog is the holy grail of library cataloging. Over the millennia, librarians have endeavored to know and to publish where books are located in towns, states, and nations. This is the basic premise of a union catalog where "union" means unified or universal. They are used to verifying that a requested material belongs to a particular library. Interlibrary loan is impossible unless the borrowing library can find out which library holds a particular item.

The union catalog has a long history that began in ancient Sumer where the contents of libraries were written on clay tablets. In the United States, the national union catalog grew out of developments at the Library of Congress (LOC). In 1901, LOC made its catalog cards available for purchase by other libraries, which accomplished two goals. First, it forced libraries to accept a particular form and codes for their own local catalog. Second, LOC discovered which books were located in libraries all over the country. Other libraries also began to print cards similar to the LOC cards, and they sent these locally made cards to Washington. This was the beginning of a unified national catalog of materials in United States libraries.

All of the cards that LOC received before 1956 were published in a 754-volume set titled the *National Union Catalog of Pre-1956 Imprints* that can be found in research libraries across the country. This achievement was only possible with the development of several new standardizations and codes that are still used in libraries today. Machine Readable Cataloging, (MARC), developed in the 1960s at the Library of Congress, made it possible for machines to read catalogs through a series of codes. Inexpensive photographic reproduction that created high-quality copies allowed the accurate distribution of library catalog cards. Eventually, the union catalog grew too large to be published in paper. It was distributed via microfiche for a while but then the records were uploaded into an online access system. This is currently the preferred method of distribution for many union catalogs.

Cooperative Library Networks

There is a rich history of libraries cooperating over varying distances. Library cooperation can be traced back to medieval monasteries in Europe where books were lent between libraries for copying (Smith, 1993: 285). As mentioned above, Green's letter to *Library Journal* notes that some libraries in the United States were already arranged in loose lending networks by the latter half of the nineteenth century.

Many different types of library networks serve different purposes. Some cooperating libraries agree to share material acquisition budgets whereas others share online public access catalogs. Some networks are geographic. These can span various city, state, and regional boundaries.

Libraries also create networks based on common subject areas. These are usually linked through an association such as the American Theological Library Association or through a national system such as the National Library of Medicine's Network of Medical Libraries. Libraries also share a common bond based institution type. Any one library might be a member of several cooperating library networks. For example, my previous institution is located in New York City and is a member of the Metropolitan New York Library Council (Metro). The library is also a member of the regional OCLC (Online Computer Library Center) service provider, Nylink. Finally, the library is part of the theological institution and is a member of the American Theological Library Association (ATLA). Each of these networks encourages interlibrary loan among its members and each has a common interlibrary loan policy to which all members must adhere.

For the purposes of this manual, one of the most important library networks is OCLC, Inc. OCLC, originally the Ohio College Library Center, began in 1967 as a resource-sharing network of academic institutions in Ohio. Its members supported the development of a linked computer catalog and adopted the MARC record. The records of any library were available to all member institutions. The original Ohio network expanded outside of state bounds in 1977 and changed its name to OCLC, Inc. Now known as OCLC, Online Computer Library Center, Inc., the library service organization has more than 69,000 member libraries; the online union catalog, WorldCat, has more than 110 million records. WorldCat (available at worldcat.org) is a vitally important resource for the small interlibrary loan department and is mentioned throughout the manual.

Communication Technology

Similar to the union catalog, interlibrary loan is impossible without a way for libraries to communicate with one another. Although it is more of a tool than technology, it was the postal service that first allowed interlibrary loan service to expand across the country. The postal service was the preferred form of sending transactions until the 1970s (Gilmer, 1994).

It is well known that communication technology changes rapidly and ILL service is directly affected by these changes. The "Interlibrary Loan" entry in a 1974 encyclopedia discusses technologies that were on the cutting edge 35 years ago. According to the article, the teletype machine (along with the mail service) was one of the preferred methods for sending information. The teletypewriter (TTY), now primarily used as a means of communication for the deaf, transmitted information from one typewriter to another through wires. The author of the entry notes that the tele-facsimile, or fax, was not a wholly satisfactory means of document transmission because "the cost was high, the facsimiles were of poor quality and the users did not seem to adjust to instantaneous transmission" (King and Johnson, 1974: 207). This uneasiness with instantaneous transmission would change over the next 20 years. Other technologies mentioned include cable television and laser beam television. The latter is still in development but the description of the former foreshadows the Internet.

During the 1980s and 1990s, technology streamlined ILL. Yem Siu Fong (1996) lists five technologies that converged to create a more efficient model for interlibrary loan. First, electronic conversion allowed text to move from one format to another. Next, storage technologies such as floppy disks and CD-ROMS permitted more digital information to be stored in smaller spaces. Third, communication technologies allowed digital formats to transfer from one computer to another. One of the most significant is the

Multipurpose Internet Mail Extension (MIME), which allows users to attach various document formats to e-mail. Fourth, workstation technologies, including the ubiquitous desktop computer, were built around a flexible, open architecture. Finally, hardcopy production such as printers improved (Fong, 1996).

These changes led directly to the first International Standards Organization ILL protocols that stipulated the rules for sending ILL messages between computers. The protocols were primarily used in Canada but were reinvigorated in the United States by the North American Interlibrary Loan/Document Delivery Project (NAILDD). NAILDD, an initiative started in 1993 by the Association of Research Libraries, focused on designing ILL systems that would make interlibrary loans more efficient. Other technological changes included the use of electronic requests and OCLC's development of a one-step verification process.

Perhaps the most significant changes came in the area of document delivery. Not only could requests be sent electronically, the actual item requested could be sent to the user's desktop. Electronic citation databases, first on CD-ROM and then online, allow users to have access to thousands of journal and book titles without initiating an ILL request. These systems are also used for fee-based document delivery supplies such as ProQuest UMI or the University of Texas at Arlington's UnCover.

The advancements in Internet and the personal computer technology are two of the greatest communication achievements of the late twentieth century. Their combined impact on interlibrary loan and document delivery cannot be underestimated. Commercially packaged software has allowed research libraries to process hundreds of thousands of ILL transactions per year. Articles are delivered directly from the lending library to the requestor's desktop. Requests can be sent over the Internet and forms no longer need to be filled out by hand. These changes have revolutionized the speed and accuracy of interlibrary loan services.

Why Provide Interlibrary Loan and Document Delivery?

Interlibrary loan is an expensive and time-consuming service, and in the days of budget cuts and layoffs, ILL is a low-visibility budget line that can be cut without a lot of public fallout. But should a library consider doing this? Why bother providing interlibrary loan and document delivery?

The best answer is that it is a vital service that helps patrons fulfill their information requirements. As Boucher noted (1997: 3), "no library can be completely self-sufficient in meeting the needs of its patrons." This is even more applicable in the beginning of the twenty-first century. With the explosion of information in both electronic and print formats, it is impossible for any library to provide all of the resources a patron might want or need. This is true even if a library is very large and its patron base is small and specialized. At some point a patron will ask a question at the reference desk for which the library has no material.

Another common reason given for reducing interlibrary loan is the proliferation of information on the Internet. If everything is available on the Web, especially through Google Books, why should any budget money go into borrowing materials from other libraries? It is true that the Internet can reduce the number of ILL transactions. Many materials are freely available on the Web and I recommend in later chapters that staff members check the Web before putting through a request. However, "everything" is not available on the Internet. The articles that patrons are looking for are often only available in the so-called "deep Web." Google Books is a wonderful resource, but the copyright policies that govern what it can and cannot display often make its scans useless for researchers.

Another reason that might be given for not providing interlibrary loan is that patrons can get their own materials. Although undoubtedly true in some cases, sometimes the resources patrons need are too far away for this to be a feasible solution. Also, patrons do not make cooperative agreements with other institutions, which can often lower the cost per item, so requiring individuals to find their own materials might not be cost-effective in the long run.

Finally, providing excellent ILL service is a good public relations move for libraries. Many patrons do not know that a library can provide materials located across the country. At some point, many staff members have encountered the familiar exchange when the patron exclaims, "You can do that? I don't have to go there to read it?" These exchanges can be helpful for the library when referendums are up for a vote.

Interlibrary loan is often one of the only services through which libraries maintain cooperative agreements. When an individual library offers interlibrary loan, it immediately becomes a member of the wider library community with a stake in the activities of the libraries from which they borrow and to which they supply.

Although there are many arguments for reducing or eliminating interlibrary loan, this should be considered only as a last resort. ILL can be provided cheaply and efficiently while maintaining high customer service standards. This manual offers many suggestions that will allow even the smallest library to provide ILL.

Basis for Best Practices in the Small Library

The term "best practices," first introduced in 1984, is borrowed from the business world. The *Dictionary for Library and Information Studies* defines them as procedures that "when properly applied consistently yield superior results and are therefore used as reference points in evaluating the effectiveness of alternative methods of accomplishing the same task. Best practices are identified by examining the empirical evidence of success" (Reitz, 2004: 66). This definition is quoted at length because "best practices" is a popular buzzword that is thrown around but rarely explained. People tout that they employ "best practices" but never explain where the best practices originated.

Best practices can best be understood as a type of action research. Usually advanced by practitioners in a field, they develop when people decide to apply a theory to a problem and evaluate the outcome. Best practices can be based on empirical research but they often arise through trial and error.

The short history of interlibrary loan given previously hints at the importance of using and publishing best practices in library service. Each time the American Library Association or the Association of College and Research Libraries adopted a new code, it was ignored by practitioners. The early codes described an ideal situation, not interlibrary loan as it was practiced by librarians. Restrictions on what could be circulated and to whom were based on idyllic notions of elite education. (Why these codes were adopted by the associations in the first place is a question for another time.) In the end, state and local policies grew out of best practices. Eventually the national organizations had to recognize the practicality of the locally grown procedures.

How do these best practices develop in library science? In general, they grow out of two areas: research studies and case studies. Large library networks such as the Association of Research Libraries (ARL) or the American Library Association invest time and money into studying library service outcomes. These studies are often funded by such national organizations such as the Institute for Museum and Library Services (IMLS).

The ARL, in particular, is interested in making interlibrary loan more efficient and cost-effective because its members are the principal users and suppliers of the service. One study used frequently through this manual found that patron-initiated ILL transactions were more cost-effective than those that were mediated by members of the library staff. Some of the studies conducted by the ALA's Association of College and Research Libraries Division were also mentioned in the previous brief history of ILL.

Case studies are ubiquitous in library science literature. They are often dismissed as "how we did it" articles but when they are aggregated, they provide justification for implementing tested theories that have been proven to work.

Best Practices in ILL

Best practices in interlibrary loan are determined by experts in the field. These are people who have worked as ILL librarians for a significant time and who have conducted the studies mentioned previously. As a field of specialization in library service, inter-library loan librarians maintain their own professional standards. There are two peer-reviewed journals that publish current infor-mation in the field: *Interlending and Document Supply* and the *Journal for Interlibrary Loan, Document Delivery & Electronic Reserve*. Interlibrary loan librarians also maintain their own e-mail discussion lists such as ILL-L and ILLiad-L for disseminating ideas and discussing problems.

Modifying Best Practices for the Small Department

One of the problems with many best practices in interlibrary loan is that they are usually developed for larger libraries. This makes sense because large libraries are major stakeholders in ILL. These practices usually assume that an institution's ILL budget will in-clude certain baseline expenditures such as a fully-staffed depart-ment and recent technology. It is often difficult for small organizations to match these overhead costs.

It is possible, however, to adapt best practices for any situation. For example, most integrated interlibrary services include some sort of program that "pushes" requests to the lending ILL librar-ian. If a small library cannot afford such a service, what resources can it use to mimic it? If someone on staff is handy with computer programming, one could add a push script to the online request form. Or, if this is too complicated, the librarian could simply set up a daily task reminder to check the request queue on his or her personal information task software. No matter what method is used, requests are sent in a timely manner and the task is accomplished.

This example illustrates the basis for modifying best practices in this book—what is the best way to complete any given task in interlibrary loan efficiently and cheaply without using expensive proprietary software and without sacrificing customer service. Having provided ILL for a small library for five years, I will use several methods for these modifications. One source of methods will be techniques developed on the job. In addition to these locally developed methods, I discuss techniques used by other libraries that increase efficiency. Descriptions of these techniques are from two sources: an informal, preliminary survey of small ILL departments and a more formal follow-up study.

The following chapter focuses on how small interlibrary loan departments differ from large ones and the trade-offs that libraries must make when interlibrary loan services are constrained by small budgets and staff time.

References

American Library Association. 2008a. *Interlibrary Loan Code for the United States.* Available: www.ala.org/ala/mgrps/divs/rusa/resources/guidelines/interlibrary.cfm (accessed July 30, 2009).

American Library Association. 2008b. *Interlibrary Loan Code for the United States Explanatory Supplement.* Available: www.ala.org/ala/mgrps/divs/rusa/resources/guidelines/interlibraryloancode.cfm (accessed July 30, 2009).

Boucher, Virginia. 1997. *Interlibrary Loan Practices Handbook.* Chicago: American Library Association.

Fong, Yem Siu. 1996. "From Paper Forms to Electronic Transmission: The Evolution of Interlibrary Loan Electronic Technologies." In *Managing Resource Sharing in the Electronic Age,* edited by Amy Chang and Mary E. Jackson. New York: AMS Press.

Gilmer, Lois C. 1994. *Interlibrary Loan: Theory and Management.* Englewood, CO: Libraries Unlimited.

Green, Samuel. 1876. "The Lending of Books to One Another by Libraries."*American Library Journal* 1 (September): 15–16.

Hilyer, Lee Andrew. 2006. *Interlibrary Loan and Document Delivery: Best Practices for Operating and Managing Interlibrary Loan Services in All Libraries.* Binghamton, NY: The Haworth Press.

Jackson, Mary E. 1997. "The Application of the ILL Protocol to Existing ILL Systems." Paper presented at the 1997 IFLA Conference ILL Protocol Standard: Interlibrary Loan in Open Networked Environment, September 2. Available: www.ifla .org (accessed October 5, 2008).

King, Geraldine, and Herbert F. Johnson. 1974. "Interlibrary Loan (ILL)." In *Encyclopedia of Library and Information Science,* edited by Allen Kent and Harold Lancour. New York: M. Dekker.

Ranganathan, S.R. 1957. *The Five Laws of Library Science.* Madras: The Madras Library Association.

Reitz, Joan M. 2004. *Dictionary for Library and Information Science.* Englewood, CO: Libraries Unlimited.

Smith, Malcolm. 1993. "Resource Sharing." In *World Encyclopedia of Library and Information Science,* edited by Robert Wedgeworth. Chicago: American Library Association.

Wright, Walter W. 1952. "Interlibrary Loan—Smothered in Tradition." *College and Research Libraries.* 13 (October): 322–336.

2

Special Topics for Small ILL and Document Delivery Departments

When I began a new job as a reference librarian, one of the duties on a long list of responsibilities was "conduct interlibrary loan." The library used WorldCat Resource Sharing and was a member of some library networks, but little information was available on policies and procedures. The training can only be described as cursory. It took an entire work day to complete just a few requests—a workday that included other tasks such as answering questions at the reference desk and weeding the reference section.

This situation would probably never occur in a large library. Large departments often have professional librarians with the title "Interlibrary Loan Librarian" whose primary job responsibility is to supervise other workers, some of whom specialize in lending or borrowing procedures. It might take all day for staff in a large interlibrary loan department to complete some difficult requests, but this is not a problem, as this would be the staff members' primary responsibility. When new workers arrive, they receive in-depth training from experienced staff.

In the small department, usually only one or two people are responsible for all aspects of interlibrary loan. Interlibrary loan is often a secondary responsibility for these staff members because their primary position is Reference Librarian or Circulation Librarian. This means that interlibrary loan can get lost in the workday shuffle.

This chapter explores some of the issues that are unique to small interlibrary loan departments. It discusses constraints small departments encounter, including staffing and budget limitations, and also explores solutions staff members can use to help ease the burden of providing interlibrary loan to their patrons. Many of the topics and suggestions come from a survey of small interlibrary loan departments (see Figure 2-1). Responses to the survey are referenced throughout the chapter.

Maximizing Limited Staff Resources

Who should conduct interlibrary loan? This is not a difficult question for large libraries to answer because they usually have an entire department dedicated to ILL. Small libraries, on the other hand, must address this question carefully by weighing many different factors, including how many transactions the library processes per year and the availability of student and/or paraprofessional workers. Deciding who should provide interlibrary loan in a small library is often a highly localized and idiosyncratic process.

The survey respondents provided a wide array of answers to the question of who handles interlibrary loan in their library. Several replied that the public services or circulation librarian conducted interlibrary loan, whereas others responded that library assistants or other paraprofessionals process requests. Some libraries used student workers under the supervision of a professional librarian. In one library, the technical services librarian provided ILL. It is clear from these responses that small interlibrary loan departments have a wide array of staffing arrangements from which to choose.

What issues should library administrators consider when staffing interlibrary loan? First, managers should focus on how many requests are received each year. More than any other factor, volume will determine how many people should be involved in ILL.

Figure 2-1: Survey of Small ILL Departments

I. Background Information

1. How many transactions (borrowing and lending) does your institution conduct per year?
   - ❑ 0–100
   - ❑ 101–200
   - ❑ 201–300
   - ❑ 301–400
   - ❑ 401–500

2. Who conducts ILL in your library?

3. How many hours do you estimate are spent on ILL per week?

II. Policy, Codes, and Copyright Law

1. Does your institution have a written ILL policy?

   - ❑ Yes
   - ❑ No

2. Does your institution follow the National Interlibrary Loan Code?

   - ❑ Yes
   - ❑ No

3. Any state or local codes?

   - ❑ Yes
   - ❑ No

4. Is someone on your library's staff familiar with copyright law as it pertains to interlibrary loan?

   - ❑ Yes
   - ❑ No

III. Networks and Technology

1. Is your institution a member of a network that facilitates interlibrary loan service?

   - ❑ Yes
   - ❑ No

2. If so, which ones? _____

3. Does your institution use computer software to manage ILL requests?

   - ❑ Yes
   - ❑ No

(continued)

(continued)

4. If so, which one? If not, what do you use instead? _____
_____

IV. Charging and Fees

1. Does your institution charge patrons for service?

    ❑ Yes
    ❑ No

2. If so, how much are the fees? _____

3. Does your institution charge other institutions for borrowing?

    ❑ Yes
    ❑ No

4. If so, what do you charge? _____

5. How does your institution keep track of invoices? _____

V. Special Issues

1. Do you believe that there are any special issues that confront small interlibrary loan departments that might not be found in a larger department?

    ❑ Yes
    ❑ No

2. If so, what are they? _____

3. Is there anything you would like to add? _____
_____

Second, administrators should consider how many hours are spent on interlibrary loan each week. Sometimes this correlates with volume and sometimes it does not. Perhaps the department receives only a few requests, but they are difficult to process. Managers should talk to staff to find out if the amount of time spent on interlibrary loan impedes the completion of other tasks.

Above all, administrators must decide what staffing arrangement works for the library's current transaction volume and workflow. Strategies that worked in the past might not work in the future. Interlibrary loan services within a given library can change over time and staffing should change with them.

For many small departments it makes sense to have a public services librarian at least supervise ILL even if he or she does not process requests regularly. In all cases, unless only one person works in the library, more than one staff member should be familiar with interlibrary loan procedures. As Morris notes in his editorial on ILL policy, "every job in a library should be shared by at least two people; libraries should not shut down operations . . . because one person is out" (Morris, 2005: 2). This is particularly important for local patron borrowing requests. It is simply poor customer service to tell patrons that they cannot borrow items for two weeks because the ILL person is on vacation.

No matter how a department is staffed, managers should ensure that interlibrary loan never becomes overly burdensome for the people who are conducting it. If staff members cannot process most requests in a timely manner, perhaps the staffing of the department needs to be reevaluated. This is particularly true if staff have trouble completing patrons' borrowing requests within a reasonable amount of time.

Time Management with Minimal Staff

Time management is a major issue of concern for the small interlibrary loan departments. The time that it takes to process requests can be surprisingly long. This is particularly true when requests are difficult to find or require extensive scanning or photocopying. Most respondents to the survey noted that they spent between 5 and 15 hours per week on ILL, although some spent as little as one hour and one spent as much 30 hours per week.

In small departments where the reference or circulation librarian conducts interlibrary loan, managing the time spent on interlibrary loan is of primary importance. Even though ILL is an important aspect of public services, personnel who fulfill other roles cannot devote substantial time to processing requests. Individual staff members must decide how best to divide their time between interlibrary loan and other duties. However, certain time management ideas can help staff members manage their time more efficiently. For example, workers may want to consider always processing borrowing requests from local patrons before moving on to lending requests from other institutions. This ensures that local patrons' needs are met no matter what other tasks might need to be completed. Chapters 6 and 7 include more suggestions on how to employ time management strategies in small interlibrary loan departments.

Budget Challenges for Finite Funds

Budgeting for interlibrary loan is also a major concern for small departments. As with most issues in libraries, budgeting is an entirely localized process. In his book on best practices in interlibrary loan, Lee Andrew Hilyer (2006) notes that managing ILL services includes both direct costs such as the fees that other libraries charge and indirect costs such as staff time, postage, and supplies. This section discusses some suggestions for managers of small interlibrary loan departments to consider when budgeting for ILL services.

Charging Patrons

Should small interlibrary loan departments charge patrons fees for the borrowing? This is a difficult question to answer. Many small libraries do not have enough money to subsidize interlibrary loans. However, if at all possible, library administration should consider not charging patron borrowing fees.

There are several reasons for this recommendation. First, charging nominal fees to patrons often does not cover the actual cost of interlibrary loan. Charging patrons only $5.00 or $10.00 does not come close to covering costs of processing, shipping, supplies, and the supplying library's fees. Second, collecting fees can consume quite a bit of staff time. Unless fees are collected at the time requests are made or the library has some other established billing system in place, the time spent sending patrons bills will probably outweigh the fee. Collecting fees from patrons can greatly decrease the department's efficiency. Finally, not charging fees can increase goodwill with patrons. Many librarians can attest to the happy look on patrons' faces when they find out that they can receive interlibrary loan for free.

Most survey respondents indicated that they did not charge patron borrowing fees but noted that they pass on any charges that are above a certain amount. If the fee is within the amount that the patron is willing to pay, when is the money collected? Before the request is sent to the supplying library? If there is a per page fee, staff members must calculate how many pages are requested to determine if it is more than the patron is willing to pay. Molly Murphy and Yang Lin note in their article that these procedures, including "determining cost, notifying patrons waiting for responses, reordering items—often add . . . weeks to the borrowing process" (Murphy and Lin, 1996: 135). They also note that fully subsidizing patron borrowing eliminates the need for patrons to determine the relative importance of materials based on their willingness (and ability) to pay for them.

For many small interlibrary departments it is easier to simply process the request. Patrons will receive their materials faster and staff time will not be wasted following up on $10.00 charges. If small departments must charge because of budgetary constraints, fees should be as easy to calculate as possible. Procedures for charging and collecting patron fees are further discussed in Chapter 7.

Charging Borrowing Libraries

It is far easier for small departments to charge borrowing libraries instead of charging patrons. These fees should also be carefully evaluated. Small libraries are encouraged to join cooperating networks that will lower the overall cost of interlibrary loan. Many of these networks include free or reduced cost interlibrary loan. Even when most of a library's borrowing requests are filled through these networks, there should still be adequate budget for postage and supplies.

Institutions outside of these networks should be charged a reasonable rate, preferably one that covers at least some of the costs associated with processing and shipping materials. Some libraries may choose to charge whatever the borrowing library charges for lending. At other libraries, borrowing institutions might be charged a fee based on the type of institution that is requesting the materials.

It is tempting for small institutions to charge borrowing institutions only for postage; however, this is often more trouble than it is worth. To understand why, it might be helpful to consider the following situation that took place when I worked as a reference librarian. A request was sent out through WorldCat Resource Sharing (WCRS) for a book at a nearby library. A few days later, I received a letter in the mail that included a printout of the WCRS request indicating that the first supplying library in the lending string charged for postage. Before I had time to respond (the answer would have been No), the book arrived in the mail. The supplying library did not include an invoice for the postage charge of $2.40. Once the patron had finished with the book, I had a dilemma: how should the library pay for postage? The business office refused to cut checks for such a small amount and sending cash in the mail seemed unwise. In the end, I sent the book back to the supplying library with three $1.00 stamps to cover not only the cost of the book but also the initial letter plus a little extra.

Would the supplying library actually use the stamps for ILL postage? Probably not, because the book had been packaged in a mailer stamped by machine. In any case, the supplying library generated quite a bit of work for its own and the borrowing library's staff members for a small amount of money. It would have been much simpler to mark the request as "Conditional" and indicate in WCRS that they charged for postage and then add the charge to ILL Fee Management (IFM), or a staff member at the supplying library could have sent an e-mail or called to let me know about the charge.

Small interlibrary loan departments should consider charging for postage only if the borrowing library requests that the materials be delivered through a special service. For some small departments this might include delivery through commercial shipping services such as FedEx and UPS. As discussed in Chapter 6, most returnable materials should be sent as cheaply as possible.

Billing and IFM

If small interlibrary loan departments choose to charge patrons, administration might want to consider adding fees to patrons' general records in the integrated library system. If the department charges borrowing libraries and the library is not a member of WorldCat Resource Sharing, invoices should be sent via e-mail whenever possible. If the library does use WCRS however, invoices should not be used at all. Small interlibrary loan departments should use OCLC's IFM whenever possible.

First developed in the mid 1990s, IFM eliminates the need for invoicing and collecting payments. IFM appears as two separate charges on the monthly OCLC bill. First, the monthly bill is debited when the supplying library charges the borrowing library a fee. Second, the bill is credited when the library supplies materials to a borrowing library and charges a fee (Boucher, 1997). OCLC also charges an administrative fee for completed IFM transactions that appears in the monthly debits for borrowing.

These charges are assessed within the OCLC WCRS request and are always optional. IFM is a fairly straightforward system to use:

1. The Borrower offers to make IFM payment to the Lender by entering a dollar amount in the Maximum Cost field, and clicking the ILL Fee Management (IFM) check box.

2. The Lender accepts the offer by entering the same or a lesser dollar amount in the Lending Charges field, and clicking the IFM check box.
3. The OCLC system matches these two fields and activates ILL Fee Management when the Borrower updates the request to *Received*. (OCLC, 2008)

Note that IFM is entirely optional—if an amount is not entered in the Lending Charges field, no fees are assessed. This means that IFM can support cooperating network agreements that include free interlibrary loan. Boucher makes note of two advantages to using IFM: "the system avoids individual invoices and presents an invoice that the library is already used to paying" (Boucher, 1997: 56).

Small interlibrary loan departments should use IFM and eliminate invoices if at all possible. In some ways, invoices are a luxury that only large ILL departments can afford. Small departments should not waste staff time producing and following up on invoices when an extremely attractive alternative exists in the form of IFM.

Technology in Small Libraries

One of the major limitations for small interlibrary loan departments is access to technology. Small libraries often have small budgets and most of the budget must go to paying salaries and buying materials. Although small institutions usually have some technology, including computer workstations and an integrated library system (ILS), they often lack adequate information technology support.

In an article on rural libraries, Joseph Anderson notes that "many communities simply don't have people with technical expertise" (Anderson, 2006). Even though small libraries may be located in areas that do have people with IT experience, they may be unable to pay computer support workers a competitive salary. Anderson writes that "when you can afford to pay $7 an hour and your local tech person can make $50 or more from his other clients, you've got a problem" (Anderson, 2006).

This lack of IT support is exacerbated in interlibrary loan. Almost all of the improvements in efficiency in the ILL are technologically based. The development of the interlibrary loan management system (IMS) has made almost all aspects of ILL entirely paperless, including sending and receiving requests, tracking materials, notifying patrons, and maintaining statistics. Lee Andrew Hilyer (2006) notes that IMS also requires support from system administrators with advanced technological expertise. Many small libraries cannot afford these extra costs. This does not mean that small interlibrary loan departments do not use any technology at all; they often cobble together systems that mimic the functions of full-featured IMS. Chapters 8 and 9 of this manual discuss commercial ILL technology and suggestions for developing a paperless ILL department without spending a lot of money.

WorldCat Resource Sharing

OCLC's WCRS is properly classified as a bibliographic utility; however, it can also function as a limited-feature IMS and as a kind of library network. It was originally developed to facilitate sharing materials that were found in OCLC's union catalog WorldCat. Over time, OCLC has greatly enhanced WCRS's features, adding functions such as the interlibrary loan fee management (IFM) system, integration with FirstSearch, and Direct Request which is discussed below. More than 9,000 libraries around the world use WCRS.

It is highly recommended that small interlibrary loan departments subscribe to WCRS if at all possible. OCLC charges an annual subscription fee, but the utility does not require any special equipment or onsite information technology support. The utility has many different features that help interlibrary loan departments of any size improve efficiency. Many of the suggestions through-out this manual will refer to WCRS procedures.

Cooperating Library Networks

As mentioned in the introductory chapter, cooperating library net-works (also known as consortia) have existed in the United States for quite awhile. Small libraries should take advantage of these networks whenever possible. Networks can be based on many dif-ferent characteristics including type of library, geographical prox-imity, or even a shared interest in allowing patrons to have access to as many materials as possible. The survey respondents be-longed to a wide variety of networks including TEXNET, CARLI, and Amigos.

The agreements between cooperating libraries can vary widely. Some networks allow for free lending and borrowing, while oth-ers offer these services for a reduced fee. Some consortia add mes-senger delivery to their agreements while others set up shared scanning services. In all cases, ILL staff should be familiar with the terms of the consortial agreements to which the library be-longs.

Libraries Very Interested in Sharing (LVIS)

Libraries Very Interested in Sharing (LVIS) (accessed 2009) de-serves special mention because it is a nationwide network that any library can join. LVIS began in 1993 when libraries in Illinois and Missouri decided to begin a free interlibrary loan network. It ex-panded to libraries nationwide in 1995.

LVIS libraries agree to six provisions. Three provisions concern OCLC: the library must participate in OCLC as a Governing Mem-ber or Member, have Supplier status, and use WorldCat Resource Sharing. Two of the provisions pertain to cost: returnable materials must be provided free of charge, whereas photocopies are free up to a maximum of 30 pages. Finally, the library must agree to share resources with all LVIS members (LVIS Agreement).

LVIS is managed through OCLC's regional offices. Small interlibrary loan departments should consider joining LVIS, particularly if the library is already a member of OCLC and uses WCRS. LVIS is one of the only multi-type national sharing networks that does not require any fees to join.

Medical Libraries

In the United States, medical libraries have their own cooperating library network known as the National Network of Libraries of Medicine (NN/LM). First established in 1965, the NN/LM is divided into eight regions with the national office at the National Library of Medicine in Bethesda, Maryland. The network is arranged hierarchically with the National Library of Medicine at the top, then regional medical libraries, followed by resource and primary access libraries (Hilyer, 2006).

NN/LM has two categories of membership. Full members are health sciences libraries or information centers that meet four criteria. They must provide services including DOCLINE to health professionals, have a collection of health-related materials, be regularly staffed, and finally, they must have an Internet connection (NN/LM Documentation). Affiliate members are institutions that do not meet these four criteria.

DOCLINE is at the heart of NN/LM's interlibrary loan network. It is a Web-based interlibrary loan management system that both routes and receives requests. It can be used with Loansome Doc, an unmediated document ordering service. Both DOCLINE and Loansome Doc are more fully discussed in Chapter 8.

Reciprocal Agreements

Reciprocal agreements are library-to-library arrangements that are more comprehensive than consortial agreements. The terms are arranged on a smaller scale, so libraries can add provisions that they might not be able to include in consortial networks.

Small interlibrary loan departments are encouraged to enter reciprocal agreements that include not only free interlibrary loan services but also incorporate reciprocal borrowing by patrons. This is particularly advantageous if the libraries are near one another. An example of a reciprocal agreement can be found in Figure 2-2.

As discussed in Chapter 6, patrons should be encouraged to use other libraries in the area, especially if they can borrow materials directly from these libraries. This places the burden for getting these materials on the patrons rather than on interlibrary loan staff members.

Unmediated ILL

The two types of interlibrary borrowing requests start with the patron filling out some sort of request form, but the similarities end there. With mediated requests, the patron's form is sent to a library staff member who reviews it and determines which institutions will be able to supply the material. The staff member then sends out the request. In unmediated transactions, once the patron fills out the form it is immediately sent to potential supplying libraries. These potential supplying libraries are selected by the system according to profiles previously established by ILL staff. In 2004, Mary E. Jackson, along with Bruce Kingma and Tom Delaney, published a major research paper for the Association of Research Libraries that definitively proved that unmediated (also called user-initiated) ILL offered better service to patrons. "In most cases, user-initiated services have lower unit costs, higher fill rates, and faster turnaround times than medicated services . . . this study recommends moving as much mediated ILL traffic as possible to a user-initiated service, and as soon as possible" (Jackson, 2004: xi).

Figure 2-2: Reciprocal Agreement

Reading College
Read Library
Reciprocal Agreement

Reading College
Read Library
321 Main St.
Anytown, NY 10011–0022
212–123–4567
212–123–4576 (Fax)
library@readingcollege.edu
http://library.readingcollege.edu

_____ and Reading College agree to enter a reciprocal borrowing and interlibrary loan agreement.

The libraries agree to the following:

1. Patrons in good standing may check out materials free of charge from either library. Patrons must assume full responsibility for all borrowed materials. Reciprocal borrowers must follow the same rules and regulations as the library's other patrons.
2. Interlibrary book loans and photocopies at no charge.

"Revisions to this agreement may be made in writing with the consent of both libraries. Either library may terminate this agreement at any time by providing one week's written notice to the other." (Hilyer, 2006: 133)

_____
Director, Read Library, Reading College   Date

_____
Director   Date

Library:

Address:

Phone Number:

Fax:

E-mail:

Web Site:

_____
Source: This agreement template is based on an example found in Lee Andrew Hilyer's *Interlibrary Loan and Document Delivery: Best Practices for Operating and Managing Interlibrary Loan* (Appendix D). Note that the agreement covers both interlibrary loan and reciprocal borrowing. It is simply worded and does not include any legalese. The agreement should be modified to suit the needs of the cooperating libraries.

This is a difficult recommendation for many small interlibrary loan departments to follow. ILL departments use mediated transactions to monitor requests and make sure that unauthorized requests do not go through. Unmediated transactions require ILL staff members to relinquish some control of ILL to a computer. If at all possible, small interlibrary loan departments should consider taking this step particularly if the library participates in WCRS.

Setting up the parameters for user-initiated ILL takes time and thoughtful preparation. OCLC's WCRS includes an extensive Planning Guide for setting up unmediated borrowing, which is known as "Direct Request" in the system. Note that there are three Direct Request options from which to choose. OCLC defines "Direct Request" as a request that the staff does not have to physically retrieve from the patron. The first option under Direct Request is called Direct-to-Review File. This option is familiar to most ILL staff. It sends all requests from patrons to a staff review file. Many would define this option as a mediated request.

Another option is "Direct-to-Lender." With this option, requests are sent directly to a series of lenders that are previously established in the borrowing library's profile. These can be sent out in order of preference and the borrowing library can establish a profile of up to 25 potential lenders. This is a true unmediated system.

"Direct-to-Profile" is, according to OCLC, the most powerful and flexible Direct Request option. This option uses a set of library-defined profiles to determine how a request will be processed. The system works in the following manner:

1. Matches the request to a bibliographic record to gather data about language, format, age of material, etc.
2. Matches the request, including bibliographic and patron data, to your Direct Request profiles. This step looks to see if the patron's status and department make him eligible to borrow the type of material he requested.
3. Once the system finds a profile match it builds a lender string. Part of your profile specifies how many symbols

must be in the lender string for a request to be forwarded directly to the first potential lender.

4. If ILL Direct Request supplies enough lenders for your lender string, the system applies the constant data record you specified, uses the bibliographic data from the WorldCat record, generates a lender string, and sends the request to the first potential lender. (OCLC, 2008)

The WCRS Direct Request is not intuitive and it takes quite a bit of time to establish. OCLC acknowledges that it may be difficult for staff members to become accustomed to using unmediated borrowing: "Even better news is that you can phase your implementation of ILL Direct Request using the Direct-to-Profile option. You can establish a few profiles to handle your simple requests and choose that only those requests go directly to lenders—all other requests will be loaded automatically to your Review File. You can build additional profiles as you gain confidence with the system" (OCLC, 2008). Using unmediated borrowing requires quite a bit of trust on the part of interlibrary loan staff. However, it is recommended that small interlibrary loan departments consider implementing user-initiated transactions in their libraries.

Document Delivery Services

Some large libraries maintain what might be called a commercial document delivery service in which they supply articles to for-profit institutions for a hefty fee. These fees are often used to subsidize regular ILL services. This type of document delivery service is not recommended for small interlibrary loan departments as they usually do not have a full-time staff person dedicated to providing this kind of service.

It is recommended that small interlibrary loan departments plan ahead for major copying jobs. At some time, the library will receive a request to copy an entire work. In academic libraries, this might be a request for a thesis or dissertation, whereas in public libraries this request might be for a book that is out of print. In either case, staff members should know ahead of time what they will charge for such large requests. It takes significant staff time to copy such voluminous material, and these requests should be charged accordingly. Small departments are encouraged to charge both a processing and per page fee as well as any shipping costs to requesting institutions.

Ensuring Customer Service through Tradeoffs

Tradeoffs are inevitable in the small interlibrary loan department. Small libraries simply do not have the resources that are available in large libraries. Managers of small departments must decide which compromises they are willing to make while continuing to maintain excellent standards of customer service.

For some libraries this might involve charging patrons a small fee to ensure that their requests arrive more quickly. Other libraries might decide that they must hire extra help in the department to meet demand. For most small departments, one of the most prominent trade-offs will be in the area of technology.

One positive aspect of this last tradeoff is that it is more or less invisible to the patron. Patrons do not know what happens to their request after they submit it; all that matters is that they receive their materials in a timely fashion. No matter what system is cobbled together behind the scenes, patrons of small interlibrary loan departments will only see the "magic" of interlibrary loan.

References

Anderson, Joseph. 2006. "Call and Response: Rural Libraries Take on Their Challenges." Available: www.webjunction.org (accessed January 20, 2009).

Boucher, Virginia. 1997. *Interlibrary Loan Practices Handbook*. Chicago: American Library Association.

Hilyer, Lee Andrew. 2006. *Interlibrary Loan and Document Delivery: Best Practices for Operating and Managing Interlibrary Loan Services in All Libraries*. Binghamton, NY: The Haworth Press.

Jackson, M. E., with B. Kingma and T. Delaney. 2004. *Assessing ILL/DD Services: New Cost-effective Alternatives*. Washington, DC: Association of Research Libraries.

Libraries Very Interested in Sharing. *Libraries Very Interested in Sharing Documentation*. Available: www.cyberdriveillinois.com (accessed January 20, 2009).

Morris, Leslie R. 2005. "Why Your Library Should Have an Interlibrary Loan Policy and What Should be Included." *Journal of Interlibrary Loan, Document Delivery & Electronic Reserve* 4: 1–7.

Murphy, Molly, and Yang Lin. 1996. "How Much Are Customers Willing to Pay for Interlibrary Loan Service?" *Journal of Library Administration* 23: 125–139.

OCLC. 2008. *WorldCat Resource Sharing Documentation*. Dublin, OH: OCLC. Available: www.oclc.org/us/en/support/documentation/resourcesharing/ (accessed July 30, 2009).

3

Copyright Law and Interlibrary Loan for Small Libraries

Copyright and Interlibrary Loan

As mentioned in the previous chapter, it is imperative for small interlibrary loan departments to have a good policy. Most interlibrary loan policies are built upon the United States Copyright Law and the national *Interlibrary Loan Code for the United States*. Although interlibrary loan codes are voluntary, all institutions are required to follow the statutes of copyright law when providing interlibrary loan services. Failure to comply with the law leaves libraries exposed to liability and copyright infringement lawsuits.

This chapter discusses copyright law for interlibrary loan services with particular emphasis on the small interlibrary loan department. It will begin with a brief overview of what copyright is, why it exists, and its history. Next, the chapter provides an outline of the various steps required to comply with copyright law when transmitting interlibrary loan requests. As with everything else in interlibrary loan, there are different provisions for borrowing and lending materials. Voluntary interlibrary loan codes are discussed in the following chapter.

Key Issues for Copyright Law

All staff members assigned to interlibrary loan should be familiar with the basics of copyright. An overview is provided below but a thorough discussion is outside the scope of this manual. The reference list at the end of the chapter includes several helpful resources that provide a more in-depth discussion of copyright law in the United States.

Copyright law is complicated and some of its provisions are difficult to understand. In order to more clearly comprehend the overview below, it is necessary to provide some background on U.S. law. Some of this information is elementary but it will clarify many of the terms that accompany any discussion of the law, including titles, codes, and regulations. All U.S. law is based on the U.S. Constitution. The first provision for copyright law is found in Article 1, Section 8 of the Constitution. Congress passes statutory laws that become part of the U.S. Code. The copyright law is Title 17 of the U.S. Code. The various amendments to the law, such as the Digital Millennium Copyright Act and the Sonny Bono Copyright Term Extension Act, change the actual words of Title 17. That is, these amendments alter the law itself. Another area of U.S. law is the *Code of Federal Regulations* (*CFR*). These administrative laws describe how the various agencies of the executive branch will enforce the U.S. Code. The copyright code is found in Title 37 of the *Code of Federal Regulations*. Both statutory and administrative laws are legally binding. When a lawsuit is brought before the courts, it is judged on the basis of both types of law. Complete information about copyright in the United States is available at the U.S. Copyright Office Web site: www.copyright.gov.

Sometimes when Congress develops new laws or amendments, the committee responsible for the law will organize a group of advisers, often called commissions, to discuss the provisions of the new bill. In 1976, during the development of the new Copyright Act, Congress assembled the National Commission on New Technological Uses of Copyright Works (CONTU) to formulate guidelines for the new law. Unlike statutory and administrative laws, these guidelines are not legally binding.

Generally speaking, the responsibility for complying with copyright law rests with the borrowing, not the lending, institution. The term "copies" refers to how many requests the borrowing library has made and received, not how many copies the borrowing library has made and sent. Also remember that libraries and other institutions can be held liable for not complying with copyright law. *Finally, please note that I am not an attorney and any issues concerning copyright should be addressed to an individual institution's legal counsel.*

What Is Copyright?

The term "copyright" refers to the sum of its parts: who has the right to copy a work. The U.S. Code does not define "work," but this term means the "intellectual creation of an author" where "author" is broadly defined as the originator of the creation (Svenonius, 2000: 9). Copyright law is primarily concerned with "fixed" works. Works are " 'fixed' in a tangible medium of expression when [their] embodiment in a copy or phonorecord, by or under the authority of the author, is sufficiently permanent or stable to permit it to be perceived, reproduced, or otherwise communicated for a period of more than transitory duration" (*Copyright Law of the United States*, Title 17: Section 101). Certain things, including ideas and concepts, cannot be copyrighted. Works do not have to be registered with the U.S. Copyright Office (www.copyright .gov) to be protected by copyright law. Works that are fixed but not covered by copyright law are in the public domain and may be copied freely.

Copyright generally belongs to either the creator of a work or its publisher. It exists for two reasons that can sometimes come into conflict: for the benefit of society and for the protection of creators. Copyright law is based on the idea that society gains when creators can profit from their work. It is similar to rights attached to property but not as easy to grasp as the works are not always as tangible as real property. By discouraging people from exploiting works, copyright encourages creators to write, compose, sculpt, paint, etc. Interlibrary loan staff are often on the forefront of the conflicts that accompany copyright law. Usually patrons request articles for scholarly research or educational purposes and these might be considered as motivations that work for the benefit of society. But how does a staff person balance this knowledge with the rights of the creator of a work? The history of copyright law demonstrates that this tension is not a new phenomenon.

History and Overview of Copyright Law

Copyright law originated in Renaissance Italy where printers held the right to copy works. With the development of the printing press, copyright law spread across Europe, eventually reaching England. The Licensing Act of 1662 gave printers in the kingdom monopoly over publishing. The act lapsed in 1665, but in 1710 Parliament passed the Statute of Queen Anne. This statute, which is the basis of modern copyright, transferred copyright ownership from printers to authors and established a fixed term for copyright protection (Gilmer, 1994).

The English colonies in North America followed the Statute of Anne until the Revolution. As mentioned previously, Article 1, Section 8, of the U.S. Constitution provides for copyright protection: "The Congress shall have Power . . . To promote the Progress of Science and useful Arts, by securing for limited Times to Authors and Inventors the exclusive Right to their respective Writings and Discoveries." However, from the end of the war until 1790, each state passed its own laws that were often difficult to enforce. In that year, the First Congress passed the Copyright Act based on the Statute of Anne. This law has been revised four times—in 1831, 1870, 1909, and 1976.

Meanwhile, a different type of copyright law, emphasizing the rights of the author, developed in continental Europe. The Berne

Convention of 1886 "established mutually satisfactory uniform copyright law to replace the need for spate registration in every country" (ARL Timeline, accessed 2008). The United States did not sign the treaty until over one hundred years later in 1988. In 1893, two small bureaus combined to form the United International Bureaux for the Protection of Intellectual Property (BIRPI). One of these grew out of the Paris Convention to Protect Industrial Property and the other grew out of the aforementioned Berne Convention. In 1967, BIRPI became the World Intellectual Property Organization (WIPO) and was absorbed by the United Nations in 1974. WIPO administers 24 treaties, one of which, the WIPO Copyright Treaty, was signed by the United States as the Digital Millennium Copyright Act of 1998.

Also of importance is the 1998 Copyright Term Extension Act, also known as the Sonny Bono Act. Under the 1976 law, copyright was held by a creator for a term of life plus 50 years. Under the Sonny Bono Act, this was extended to life plus 70 years. The Act also extended copyright for works published before January 1, 1978, by 20 years for a total of 95 years (Section 302–304). This standard determines the timeline for when works move into the public domain.

As mentioned previously, it is not necessary to register a work with the U.S. Copyright Office in order to be protected by copyright law. However, in order to sue for copyright infringement, works must be registered. The Copyright Office is one of the service divisions of the Library of Congress and is run by the Register of Copyrights.

The 1976 Copyright Act

The copyright code of the United States is contained in Title 17 of the U.S. Code. Its most recent revision is the 1976 Copyright Act. The revision, which was under consideration for over 20 years, was the direct result of advancements in photocopying technology. Sections 101–108 of the U.S. Code are the most pertinent for libraries and interlibrary loan. The U.S. Code has been amended several times since 1976 by the passage of bylaws such as the Digital Millennium Copyright Act and the Berne Convention Implementation Act of 1988.

As mentioned in the section on key terms, Congress convened the National Commission on New Technological Uses of Copyright Works (CONTU) in anticipation of this revision. The commission's final report consisted of several recommendations for changing the sections of the U.S. Code that related to libraries and archives. It also developed specific guidelines for interlibrary loan-related photocopying. Even though the CONTU Guidelines do not have the force of law, following the recommendations will help borrowing libraries remain within the boundaries of fair use when requesting photocopies.

Out of the seven sections of the 1976 copyright law that pertain to libraries, three apply directly to interlibrary loan. Section 106 states that the owner of the copyright has the exclusive right to reproduce his or her work. Section 107 describes the fair use doctrine. Reproduction by libraries and archives are described in section 108. According to Gilmer (1994), the laws pertaining to photocopying for interlibrary loan were the most controversial part of this section because some publishers worried that photocopying would lead to a reduction in sales. This was one of the motivations for Congress to convene the National Commission on New Technological Uses of Copyright Works (Gilmer, 1994).

Section 106: What Does Owning Copyright Mean?

Section 106 of the U.S. Code describes what the copyright owner can do with a copyrighted work. He or she can reproduce it, make derivative works, and perform or display the work publicly. The provisions described in Sections 107 and 108 are *exceptions* to the rights outlined in Section 106. Even though it is not mentioned in the code, authors of journal articles usually transfer all rights of ownership to the publisher. For interlibrary loan, this means that terms must be negotiated with the publisher of a journal rather than the author of the article.

Section 107: Fair Use

Fair use is one of the most difficult areas of copyright law to understand. It is almost impossible to work in a library setting and not hear the term used from time to time. Fair use refers to a very specific provision of the copyright law and also limits the exclusive rights of copyright owners. Section 107 of the Copyright Code states:

> Notwithstanding the provisions of sections 106 and 106A, the fair use of a copyrighted work, including such use by reproduction in copies or phonorecords or by any other means specified by that section, for purposes such as criticism, comment, news reporting, teaching (including multiple copies for classroom use), scholarship, or research, is not an infringement of copyright. In determining whether the use made of a work in any particular case is a fair use the factors to be considered shall include—
> (1) the purpose and character of the use, including whether such use is of a commercial nature or is for nonprofit educational purposes;
> (2) the nature of the copyrighted work;
> (3) the amount and substantiality of the portion used in relation to the copy-righted work as a whole; and
> (4) the effect of the use upon the potential market for or value of the copy-righted work. The fact that a work is unpublished shall not itself bar a finding of fair use if such finding is made upon consideration of all the above factors. (*Copyright Law of the United States*, Title 17: Section 107)

The doctrine of fair use is guided by the four factors enumerated in Section 17: purpose, nature, amount, and effect. Fair use attempts to clarify the limitations on the exclusive ownership rights of a copyright holder and determines when it is permissible for an institution to reproduce a copyrighted work. For most small interlibrary loan departments, following the CONTU Guidelines will help staff members remain within the boundaries of the law. Unfortunately, as described in the following, many ILL requests are not covered by the CONTU Guidelines. Because of this, all staff members should be familiar with the general outlines of the fair use doctrine.

The doctrine of fair use is not always easy to understand and its application is often cause for controversy. The explosion of new formats in the past 30 years has made the CONTU Guidelines somewhat obsolete. In 1997, the Conference on Fair Use (CONFU) failed to reach a consensus on fair use and electronic documents. CONFU did create a set of guidelines; however, as the various constituents could not agree on one set of principles, interlibrary loan departments can still follow the CONTU Guidelines.

Other guidelines for various situations that library staff may encounter in daily operations also exist, including the Fair Use Guidelines for Electronic Reserve Systems (available at www .utsystem.edu/ogc/intellectualproperty/rsrvguid.htm) and the Model Policy Concerning College and University Photocopying for Classroom, Research and Library Reserve Use (available at www.cni.org/docs/infopols/ALA.html#mpup). In his book on copyright, *Copyright Law for Librarians and Educators*, Kenneth Crews (2005) notes that these guidelines often have many problems, including a tendency to both narrowly construe the law and to create rigidity in its application. This comes out of a need for the guidelines to be acceptable to many diverse groups with competing interests. Even with these caveats, it is best for the small interlibrary loan department to follow the CONTU Guidelines because they were created under a congressional mandate and were part of the original Conference Committee Report when the copyright law was under revision (Boucher, 1997: 71). In the event of a lawsuit, staying within the guidelines will help lessen the library's liability. The doctrine of fair use is explained in further detail in the section on steps for copyright compliance.

Section 108: Photocopying

The CONTU Guidelines are also closely related to Section 108 of the copyright code. These are also exceptions to the exclusive rights listed in Section 106. Subtitled "Reproduction by libraries and archives," Section 108 describes the situations in which a library may copy a copyrighted work. Gilmer notes that Sections 107 and 108 are related but not identical. Section 107 pertains to everyone while Section 108 is only for libraries and archives (Gilmer, 1994). To be protected, per Section 108(a)(2), under this provision, libraries and archives must be open to the public and available to researchers (private libraries and constituent-only libraries are not covered). The employees of these public institutions are also specifically protected under Section 108.

Crews (2005) divides the provisions for photocopying delineated in section 108 into three different types of copies a library may make: copies for preservation, copies for private study, and copies for interlibrary loan. Section 108(g)(2) states that libraries may not participate in interlibrary loan as a substitute for purchasing a subscription to a journal or ordering a copy of a book. This is where the CONTU Guidelines come in. After an interlibrary loan department has received its quota of copies, it must evaluate other alternatives for finding the item.

Several of the administrative laws in the *Code of Federal Regulations* clarify the statutory laws listed in Section 108 of the copyright law. Libraries may not copy musical works (interpreted as a musical compositions), materials generally considered to be fine art such as pictures or sculptures, or motion pictures and audiovisual works. According to Section 108(f)(3), libraries may copy items that are not specifically prohibited including "audiovisual new programs."

The final provision in Section 108 discusses two signs and one signing statement that libraries must post to inform patrons of copyright protection and to protect both the institution and staff from lawsuits. These signs are described in detail in Title 37 in the *Code of Federal Regulations* and are discussed further in the following section.

The Borrowing Library: Steps for Compliance

Some Points to Remember

As mentioned previously, most of the burden for complying with copyright law rests with the borrowing library. Keep this in mind when reading the following steps. Also, it can be difficult to remember which party needs to know what information. I hope to ameliorate this confusion by dividing the compliance process into separate steps for the borrowing and lending institutions.

Step 1: Information for the Patron

U.S. copyright law requires that patrons be aware of the copyright code before they even make a request. This is accomplished through the signs described in Section 108. The first is the "Display Warning of Copyright." This sign tells patrons that the materials they are requesting through interlibrary loan or reproducing on a copying machine may be protected by copyright law. Most library staff and patrons are familiar with these signs as they are posted above photocopy machines; however, they also must be on display "at the place where [interlibrary loan] orders are accepted" (*Copyright Law of the United States*, Title 17: Section 108(d)(e)(2)). These notices protect the library and its staff in case of copyright infringement by the patron.

The U.S. *Code of Federal Regulations*, Title 37, Section 201.14(c), states that the sign shall be printed on heavy paper or other durable material in type at least 18 points in size, and shall be displayed prominently, in such manner and location as to be clearly visible, legible, and comprehensible to a casual observer within the immediate vicinity of the place where orders are accepted. The sign (see below) clarifies fair use for libraries under the copyright code and warns patrons that if they do not follow the code they will be held liable. It also states that libraries may refuse any requests that fall outside of the law.

NOTICE
Warning Concerning Copyright Restrictions

The copyright law of the United States (Title 17, United States Code) governs the making of photocopies or other reproductions of copyrighted material. Under certain conditions specified in the law, libraries and archives are authorized to furnish a photocopy or other reproduction.

One of these specific conditions is that the photocopy or reproduction is not to be "used for any purpose other than private study, scholarship, or research." If a user makes a request for, or later uses, a photocopy or reproduction for purposes in excess of "fair use," that user may be liable for copyright infringement.

This institution reserves the right to refuse to accept a copying order if, in its judgment, fulfillment of the order would involve violation of copyright law.

Interlibrary loan departments should place this sign near hard copy ILL request forms. The sign should also be posted near any photocopy machines as well as "VCRs, tape decks, microfilm readers, computers, printers, and any other equipment that is capable of making copies" (Crews, 2005: 78).

The second patron notification, which uses the same wording as the previous sign, appears on the request form itself. This is true even if the form is in electronic format. The U.S. Code of Federal Regulations also gives strict instructions for this Order Warning. It must be:

. . . printed within a box located prominently on the order form itself, either on the front side of the form or immediately adjacent to the space calling for the name or signature of the person using the form. The notice shall be printed in type size no smaller than that used predominantly throughout the form, and in no case shall the type size be smaller than 8 points. The notice shall be printed in such manner as to be clearly legible, comprehensible, and readily apparent to a casual reader of the form. (CFR 201.14(2))

These two "Warnings" are different from the notices placed on the copy itself. They remind the patron to think about what he or she is requesting and how they will use the item once it is in his or her possession. The first warning sign is a general reminder while, due to its placement on the form, the second warning is a signing statement. As Thomas Lipinski notes in his exhaustive book on copyright liability in libraries, "it could be argued that having the patron read and sign the warning notice containing the private use language equates to the library having no notice of 'other than private study, scholarship or research' " (Lipinski, 2006: 310). In other words, it also helps protect the library from copyright lawsuits.

These two warnings are the first ones that a patron will see. As is described later, the patron receives a third warning on the item itself. The next step for the borrowing library, however, pertains to the interlibrary loan department staff.

Step 2: Determining Copyright

Determining copyright should be straightforward, but often it is not. The requesting library does not have the item in front of them; therefore, staff members cannot look for a copyright notice on the work. As mentioned, the Sonny Bono Act (also known as the 1998 Copyright Term Extension Act) radically changed the timeline for moving works into the public domain. Most libraries use the 95-year rule: "if an item was first published more than ninety-five years ago, it is fairly safe to assume it is in the public domain" (Hilyer, 2006: 43). If the requested item is in the public domain it can be copied freely and the request may be sent out to potential lending libraries.

If an item, such as a manuscript, has been created but not published, it is even more difficult to determine if the work is in the public domain. To do so, staff must judge for themselves based on variables such as when the item was created and the life of the author. For the small interlibrary loan department, once again, it is best to take a cautious approach: if you are unsure about the copyright status of a requested item, assume that the item is covered by copyright.

Once a requested item is determined to be covered by the copyright law, staff members must then decide if it can be copied under the doctrine of fair use.

Step 3: Determining Fair Use

The CONTU Guidelines work according to a general rule of thumb known as the "Rule of 5" Guideline:

- 1—One calendar year
- 1—One periodical title
- 5—Five articles
- 5—Five years

During one calendar year, a library may request and receive five articles from one periodical title published within the past five years. If the request falls within these parameters, order the article.

There are several important issues to remember when using the guidelines. First, the 1–1–5–5 guidelines refer to the five years prior to the date of the request. Second, the five articles do not refer to individual periodical titles, so if two people request and receive the same article, both requests count individually toward the five. Third, the final "5" illustrates one of the limitations of the CONTU Guidelines—it does not cover periodicals older than five years. Fourth, the guidelines refer to articles that are both requested and *received*. Finally, the guidelines only address articles in periodicals not chapters in books or other materials.

If the request falls out of the CONTU Guidelines then the staff member must use his or her judgment to determine fair use. This is where the aforementioned purpose, nature, amount, and effect come in. Purpose simply means "What will the patron do with the copied item?" Will it be used commercially or in a nonprofit setting for education or research? According to Kenneth Crews (2005) in *Copyright Law Librarians and Educators*, the law clearly favors nonprofit, educational use. However, the nature of the institution (i.e., whether the institution is nonprofit public or academic library) does not mean that the item can be requested under fair use law even if the "purpose" factor is fulfilled. All four factors must be weighed together.

The second factor, the nature of the work, refers to the "characteristics and qualities" of the work (Crews, 2005: 46). Interestingly, Crews notes that courts tend to be more lenient with works of nonfiction rather than fiction. This is due to the belief that non-fiction works are "exactly the types of works for which fair use can have the most meaning" (Crews, 2005: 46). Inhibiting their wider dissemination would impede research and creativity.

Small interlibrary loan departments, in order to ward off potential lawsuits, should copy less rather than more. There are certain occasions when an entire work can be copied but they usually relate to the availability of a copy of the work and other extenuating circumstances. The discussion of Section 108 of the copyright law mentions two circumstances where this might be permissible, including copying entire works for preservation and copying entire works for private study.

The fourth factor, effect, refers to whether the library should simply buy the item rather than requesting it through interlibrary loan. This factor does not take willingness or ability to pay into account. By "effect" the law means the effect on the market and, by extension, on the creator of the work. Crews notes that "effect" is closely linked to "purpose" but the rules are less clear in the area of education. "The hard reality is that even some educational uses have direct and adverse market consequences" (Crews, 2005: 50). This is particularly true when copying chapters in a book.

Once a staff member decides that the request is within the boundaries of fair use, he or she can send it out for fulfillment. If it is not, the staff member has several choices. In her handbook, Boucher (1997) lists 11 options for obtaining items outside of interlibrary loan. For most small departments, it makes sense to pay for the article directly from the publisher, pay royalties through the Copyright Clearance Center (www.copyright.com), or direct the patron to another library that owns the item. The Copyright Clearance Center is a nonprofit company that connects libraries and other institutions with publishers to facilitate the payment of licensing fees. The center's Pay-Per-Use Permission Service is one of the easiest ways to pay royalty and licensing fees.

Step 4: Showing Compliance

Copyright compliance must be indicated on the request form that is sent to the lending library. Both hard copy and electronic request forms must have two checkboxes on them; one indicates compliance with the copyright guidelines, and the other indicates compliance with the copyright law.

These two types of compliance are usually indicated by the initialisms CCG (conforms to copyright guidelines) and CCL (conforms to copyright law). "Copyright guidelines" refers to the CONTU Guidelines outlined previously. Therefore, no matter what, staff members cannot check CCG if the request is for an article published more than five years ago. If the request falls outside of the guidelines but is within the boundaries of fair use (i.e., copyright law), check the CCL box. If the library is paying royalty fees through the Copyright Clearance Center or some other entity, CCL should be checked. Just to reiterate, staff *must* check one of the two boxes to indicate compliance.

Step 5: Retain Records

According the CONTU Guidelines, all filled requests for copies should be retained for the current year plus the previous three years. This is based on the calendar year and not the academic year. Requests for loans do not need to be saved. Boucher notes that these records provide valuable information when allocating acquisition budgets because "such records can show demonstrated rather than estimated use by a number of patrons for a particular title" (Boucher, 1997: 75).

The Lending Library: Steps for Compliance

Step 1: Check for Copyright Compliance

The lending library must ensure that the borrowing library has checked either the CCG or the CCL. Remember that the burden for copyright compliance falls on the borrowing library. Library staff may choose not to fulfill a request if there is no indication of compliance. If the request is clearly falls outside of copyright law, the lending library may reject the request. For example, if the request is for an entire work but there is no indication that it is for a replacement copy, the request should not be filled. As Boucher notes, "occasionally it is necessary to return a request to the borrowing library even though a representation is made, because it is obvious that the borrowing library does not understand the law" (Boucher, 1997: 76).

Step 2: Indicate Copyright Protection

With the passage of the Digital Millennium Copyright Act (DMCA), lending libraries are required to include a copy of the original copyright notice with the requested item. For most journal articles, copyright notice is provided on the first page of each article. For books, copyright notice is generally on the verso of the title page. Since the passage of the 1978 Copyright Act, libraries have stamped the following notice on copied materials:

> NOTICE: This material may be protected by Copyright Law (Title 17 U.S.C.)

After the DMCA passed, the Association of Research Libraries requested legal clarification regarding the notice of copyright provisions in the law. Arnold Lutzker, an attorney in Washington, DC, provided a memorandum that states that if the supplying library cannot provide the original copyright notice, then stamping the copy with the previous message is sufficient to comply with the law (Lutzker, 1999).

Understanding Copyright Law

The discussion presented here is a brief overview of copyright law, as a more thorough discussion is outside the scope of this manual. It is hoped that all staff members who work in interlibrary loan will familiarize themselves with some of the more relevant aspects of copyright law. The steps outlined here should provide a good starting point, but it is inevitable that interlibrary loan staff will encounter problematic requests.

As mentioned previously, copyright law consists of both statutory and administrative laws that must be followed by all libraries. The codes discussed in the next chapter are voluntary guidelines that each individual institution can choose to follow or not.

References

Association of Research Libraries. "Copyright Timeline: A History of Copyright in the United States." Available: www

.arl.org/pp/ppcopyright/copyresources/copytimeline.shtml (accessed July 30, 2009).

Boucher, Virginia. 1997. *Interlibrary Loan Practices Handbook.* Chicago: American Library Association.

Code of Federal Regulations, Title 37, Patents, Trademarks, and Copyrights. Available: www.copyright.gov/title37/ (accessed July 30, 2009).

Copyright Law of the United States, Title 17, §§101, 106–108. 1976. Available: www.copyright.gov/title17/ (accessed July 30, 2009).

Crews, Kenneth D. 2005. *Copyright Law for Librarians and Educators: Creative Strategies and Practical Solutions.* Chicago: American Library Association.

Gilmer, Lois C. 1994. *Interlibrary Loan: Theory and Management.* Englewood, CO: Libraries Unlimited.

Hilyer, Lee Andrew. 2006. *Interlibrary Loan and Document Delivery: Best Practices for Operating and Managing Interlibrary Loan Services in All Libraries.* Binghamton, NY: The Haworth Press.

Lipinski, Thomas A. 2006. *The Complete Copyright Liability Handbook for Librarians and Educators.* New York: Neal-Schuman.

Lutzker, Arnold P. 1999. "Memorandum." Available: www.arl .org/ala/aboutala/offices/wo/woissues/copyrightb/federal legislation/dmca/analysis.pdf (accessed July 30, 2009).

National Commission on New Technological Uses of Copyright Works. 1978. "CONTU Guidelines on Photocopying under Interlibrary Loan Arrangements." Washington, DC: Library of Congress. Available: www.cni.org/docs/infopols/CONTU.html (accessed July 30, 2009).

Svenonius, Elaine. 2000. *The Intellectual Foundation of Information Organization.* Cambridge: MIT Press.

U.S. Constitution, Article 1, Section 8: The Legislative Branch, Powers of Congress. Available: www.usconstitution.net/xconst _A1Sec8.html (accessed July 30, 2009).

4

Interlibrary Loan Codes

ILL Governing Codes

Many aspects of librarianship are governed by codes. One of the most familiar is the *Code of Ethics of the American Library Association*. Recently amended in 2008, it was developed by the American Library Association Committee on Professional Ethics. The *Code of Ethics* codifies and publicizes the "the ethical principles that guide the work of librarians, other professionals providing information services, library trustees and library staffs" (American Library Association, 2008a).

A code can be defined as a "code of practice" or "guidelines for practice." Although it may not be possible to meet every provision of the national ILL code, all departments should strive to do so. Even though the codes are not legally binding, they should be included in library policy.

Principle III of the ALA *Code of Ethics*, which pertains to library patrons' confidentiality, has come under close scrutiny over the past few years. It states that "we protect each library user's right to privacy and confidentiality with respect to information sought or received and resources consulted, borrowed, acquired or transmitted" (American Library Association, 2008a). This principle is also upheld by the national *Interlibrary Loan Code of the United States* (American Library Association, 2008b).

Chapter 1 included a brief history of the American Library Association interlibrary loan codes developed. The current code, approved in 2009, was developed by the Reference and User

Services Association (RUSA), one of the divisions of ALA. The code is freely available on the ALA Web site along with an explanatory supplement (American Library Association, 2008c).

This chapter begins with an in-depth discussion of the national library code and then briefly discusses state, local, and cooperating library codes. It reproduces the code in full with annotations written with an eye toward the code's relevance for small interlibrary loan departments. These annotations are based on both the code and the explanatory notes that accompany it. The annotations also explore some of the significant changes between the 2001 and the 2008 codes.

Interlibrary Loan Code for the United States (2008)

Introduction

The Reference and User Services Association, acting for the American Library Association in its adoption of this code recognizes that the sharing of material between libraries is an integral element in the provision of library service and believes it to be in the public interest to encourage such an exchange.

In the interest of providing quality service, libraries have an obligation to obtain material to meet the informational needs of users when local resources do not meet those needs. Interlibrary loan (ILL), a mechanism for obtaining material is essential to the vitality of all libraries.

The effectiveness of the national interlibrary loan system depends upon participation of libraries of all types and sizes.

This code establishes principles that facilitate the requesting of material by a library and the provision of loans or copies in response to those requests. In this code, "material" includes books, audiovisual materials, and other returnable items as well as copies of journal articles, book chapters, excerpts, and other nonreturnable items.

The code begins by stating that the Reference and User Services Association, which, as a division of ALA, is acting for the American Library Association in its development and adoption of the *Interlibrary Loan Code*. One of the significant differences between the 2001 and 2008 codes is the latter's acknowledgment of changes in interlibrary loan technology. The explanatory notes of the 2008 code specifically discuss modifications to the code necessitated by the ubiquity of unmediated requests and availability of full-text documents. It encourages libraries to employ "nontraditional means" of access to fulfill patron requests.

As mentioned in the brief history in Chapter 1, the question of who should use interlibrary loan services caused much controversy in the field. For many years only "serious" scholars could use the service to obtain materials. The previous revision to the code in 2001 removed the need for any judgment calls on the part of the library staff. Patrons have the right to use interlibrary loan to fulfill any information need they might have. This is important because it might be tempting for small interlibrary loan departments to reduce patron requests based on "need." However, limiting patrons in this manner is a violation of the code.

1.0 Definition

1.10   Interlibrary loan is the process by which a library requests material from, or supplies material to, another library.

The explanatory notes state that the Code only covers interlibrary loan services between two libraries, not between libraries and commercial suppliers.

2.0 Purpose

2.1   The purpose of interlibrary loan as defined by this code is to obtain, upon request of a library user, material not available in the user's local library.

For small interlibrary loan departments (which are often part of a small library), it is important to note that local library collections are intended to meet the "routine needs of users" and interlibrary loan is meant to supplement the library collection. If a small department frequently requests the same material, perhaps the institution needs to buy it for the local collection.

3.0 Scope

3.1   This code is intended to regulate the exchange of material between libraries in the United States.

3.2   Interlibrary loan transactions with libraries outside of the United States are governed by the International Federation of Library Associations and Institutions' International Lending: Principles and Guidelines for Procedure.

This guideline introduces another library association to the world of interlibrary loan. The International Federation of Library Associations and Institutions (IFLA) is an organization of libraries and other information service institutions throughout the world. The IFLA Office for International Lending and the Section on Document Delivery and Resource Sharing created interlibrary loan codes and guidelines that govern transactions between libraries in different countries.

Shipping between the United States and Canada is covered by a separate agreement between the Association of Research Libraries (ARL) and the National Library of Canada. Small interlibrary

loan departments should consider these guidelines carefully before lending materials internationally.

4.0 Responsibilities of the Requesting Library

4.1   Establish, promptly update, and make available an in-
       terlibrary borrowing policy.

A library cannot simply have a policy; it also must be a public policy. Making users aware of the library's interlibrary loan policy
will reduce misunderstandings between patrons and interlibrary
loan department staff. Chapter 4 discusses how to create a good
policy for the small interlibrary loan department.

4.2   Ensure the confidentiality of the user.

User confidentiality is an important aspect of librarianship. This
guideline reinforces Principle III of the ALA *Code of Ethics*.
However, the explanatory notes state that the user's name *can* be
included on the request given to the lending library.

4.3   Describe completely and accurately the requested ma-
       terial following accepted bibliographic practice.
4.4   Identify libraries that own the requested material and
       check and adhere to the policies of potential supplying
       libraries.

This is one of the most important skills an interlibrary loan staff
person can have. Knowing which library has an item through the
use of union catalogs and other resources, a skill discussed in
Chapter 7, is one of the most difficult aspects of interlibrary loan
service.

   The explanatory notes for this section also discuss ILL fees and
encourage the use of electronic invoicing. Information regarding

the OCLC Interlibrary Loan Fee Management system is also included in Chapter 6.

> 4.5   When no libraries can be identified as owning the needed material, requests may be sent to libraries believed likely to own the material, accompanied by an indication that ownership is not confirmed.

For small interlibrary loan departments with limited time to devote to finding materials, it is best to call the likely library before sending the request. This will save time in the long run.

> 4.6   Transmit interlibrary loan requests electronically whenever possible.

The term "electronically" refers to integrated interlibrary loan systems, not to e-mail. These systems are discussed in further detail in Chapter 8. This is probably one of the most difficult parts of the code for some small interlibrary loan departments to fulfill. As mentioned in the introduction, many smaller libraries do not have access these expensive systems. Some suggestions for meeting this guideline without spending a lot of money are provided in Chapter 9.

> 4.7   For copy requests, the requesting library must comply with the U.S. copyright law (Title 17, U.S. Code) and its accompanying guidelines.

Copyright law is the subject of Chapter 3.

> 4.8   Assume responsibility for borrowed material from the time it leaves the supplying library until it has been returned to and received by the supplying library. This includes all material shipped directly to and/or returned by the user. If damage or loss occurs, provide compensation or replacement, in accordance with the preference of the supplying library.

This is an important point. Even if the borrowing library insists that the material was returned in the mail, if it is not received by the supplying library, it is still the requesting library's responsibility to pay any fees that might be assessed.

> 4.9   Assume full responsibility for user-initiated transactions.

Unmediated requests are treated like any other—the borrowing library assumes full responsibility for the transaction.

> 4.10   Honor the due date and enforce any use restrictions specified by the supplying library. The due date is defined as the date the material is due to be checked-in at the supplying library.

According to the explanatory notes, the due date is the date that "the material must be checked in at the supplying library." It does not refer to the amount of time that a patron can use the material. Due dates for lending are explained in more detail in Chapter 6. The notes also state that all use restrictions including "library use only" and "no photocopying" must be enforced by the requesting library.

> 4.11   Request a renewal before the item is due. If the supplying library does not respond, the requesting library may assume that a renewal has been granted extending the due date by the same length of time as the original loan.
>
> 4.12   All borrowed material is subject to recall. Respond immediately if the supplying library recalls an item.

Small interlibrary loan departments often do not have easy access to expedited shipping services. However, if an item is recalled staff should make an effort to use a shipping company. The United States Postal Service also offers accelerated shipping services such as Overnight and Priority Mail.

4.13   Package material to prevent damage in shipping and comply with any special instructions stated by the supplying library.

Different shipping materials are surveyed in depth in Chapter 6. It is the borrowing library's responsibility to follow special shipping requests. The explanatory notes state that it is acceptable to reuse packing material as long as new address information is clearly marked. Tape is preferred over staples for sealing packages.

4.14   Failure to comply with the provisions of this code may be reason for suspension of service by a supplying library.

5.0 Responsibilities of the Supplying Library

5.1   Establish, promptly update, and make available an interlibrary lending policy.

The lending library also needs a clear, public policy.

5.2   Consider filling all requests for material regardless of format.

According to the explanatory notes, libraries are expected to lend material in nontraditional formats. However, it is permissible to indicate in an institution's policy that it will only do so on a case-by-case basis. This is particularly important for small interlibrary loan departments that often do not have the resources to lend newspapers or rare materials. The explanatory notes also state that libraries must be aware of and stay within the legal provisions of electronic licensing agreements.

5.3   Ensure the confidentiality of the user.

Once again supplying libraries are expected to follow Principle III of the ALA *Code of Ethics*.

> 5.4 Process requests in a timely manner that recognizes the needs of the requesting library and/or the requirements of the electronic network or transmission system being used. If unable to fill a request, respond promptly and state the reason the request cannot be filled.

Requests should be processed as quickly as possible. If an institution uses a system that pushes requests to another library, the explanatory notes recommend each library respond to the request and not allow the push to take place automatically. This is more difficult for interlibrary loan departments that do not use integrated systems. Recommendations for complying with this section of the code are discussed in Chapter 6. Also, all bills should be paid on time. The explanatory notes discourage the use of invoicing systems and recommend that libraries use electronic billing services such as OCLC's ILL Fee Management System (IFM).

> 5.5 When filling requests, send sufficient information with each item to identify the request.

Just as borrowing libraries need to supply accurate information, so do lending libraries. This saves the time of staff members on both sides of the transaction. Libraries are also encouraged to supply return mailing labels.

> 5.6 Indicate the due date and any restrictions on the use of the material and any special return packaging or shipping requirements. The due date is defined as the date the material is due to be checked in at the supplying library.

Use restrictions for materials should be clearly indicated on any documentation that accompanies the materials. The current guidelines maintain a change introduced in the 2001 revision and no longer encourage the use of the term "four weeks' use" for due dates. Supplying libraries should establish a definite due date for materials. "A supplying library might establish a due date of six (6) weeks for the purpose of providing one (1) week for shipping, four (4) weeks for use, and one (1) week for the return trip and check-in" (American Library Association, 2008c). A variation of this method for establishing due dates, which includes a longer due date in the library's integrated library system (ILS), is described in Chapter 6.

> 5.7 Ship material in a timely and efficient manner to the location specified by the requesting library. Package loaned material to prevent loss or damage in shipping. Deliver copies electronically whenever possible.

Do not send items that cannot be shipped safely and include a return address label.

> 5.8 Respond promptly to requests for renewals. If no response is sent, the requesting library may assume that a renewal has been granted extending the due date by the same length of time as the original loan.

The Explanatory Notes state that lending libraries should grant renewals whenever possible.

> 5.9 Loaned material is subject to recall at any time.

It is often difficult to receive recalled ILL materials in a timely fashion. Apparently, some libraries simply send out ILL requests for materials loaned to another library rather than trying to get the materials back. Small interlibrary loan departments may want to consider this method when users request that an item be recalled.

> 5.10 Failure to comply with the provisions of this code may lead to suspension of service to the requesting library.

Talk to the staff members at the borrowing library before suspending interlibrary loan service.

Other Interlibrary Loan Codes

Most libraries are members of several different networks, any of which might have their own interlibrary loan code. If an individual institution chooses to provide service within a particular network, it must adhere to the network's code. These codes vary but many are based on the national interlibrary loan code outlined previously. This is particularly true of state interlibrary codes. For example, Wisconsin uses the national code but supplements it with its own intrastate guidelines. These specify that it is a violation of state law to charge users for service.

All interlibrary loan staff should be familiar with the guidelines for the state in which the institution resides. These codes can be found a variety of different ways but it is easiest to begin with an Internet search. Otherwise, contact the state library association.

Other interlibrary loan codes, such as those developed for local networks or associations, should be available either directly from the governing agency or the network's Web site. These local codes supersede the national code when transmitting interlibrary loan requests within a network. Interlibrary loan departments in small libraries should also consider establishing reciprocal ILL agreements. These allow the two libraries to provide interlibrary loan service to each other at no cost to the borrowing institutions.

Conclusion

Interlibrary loan codes provide guidelines for all libraries to provide a high level of service to patrons. Although some of these standards might be difficult for small interlibrary loan departments, all institutions should attempt to follow the codes. Chapter

5 discusses how both copyright law and interlibrary loan codes are incorporated into good policy for interlibrary loan service.

References and Works Consulted

American Library Association. 2008a. *Code of Ethics of the American Library Association.* Available: www.ala.org/ala/aboutala/offices/oif/statementspols/codeofethics/codeethics.cfm (accessed July 30, 2009).

American Library Association. 2008b. *Interlibrary Loan Code for the United States.* Available: www.ala.org/ala/mgrps/divs/rusa/resources/guidelines/interlibrary.cfm (accessed July 30, 2009).

American Library Association. 2008c. *Interlibrary Loan Code for the United States Explanatory Supplement.* Available: www.ala.org/ala/mgrps/divs/rusa/resources/guidelines/interlibraryloancode.cfm (accessed July 30, 2009).

Association of Research Libraries. 1999. *Transborder Interlibrary Loan: Shipping Interlibrary Loan Materials from the U.S. to Canada.* Available: http://collectionscanada.ca/8/3/r3-649-e.html (accessed August 28, 2009).

International Federation of Library Associations. 2007. *Guidelines for Best Practice in Interlibrary Loan and Document Delivery.* Available: http://archive.ifla.org/VI/2/p3/Guidelines_ILDD-en.htm (accessed August 28, 2009).

5

General Considerations for ILL and Document Delivery Policy

Good policy is the foundation for excellent interlibrary loan and document delivery service. The process of developing policies helps staff members focus on who they want to serve and how the department will provide services for both their patrons and borrowing libraries. In an editorial titled "Why Your Library Should Have an Interlibrary Loan Policy and What Should Be Included," Leslic R. Morris, the editor of the *Journal of Interlibrary Loan, Document Delivery & Electronic Reserve*, implores all institutions that provide interlibrary loan to have a complete written policy (Morris, 2005). Morris notes that people may not read or follow the policy, but it is still necessary to have one.

This chapter discusses why written policies are important, who should write policies in a small department, and the process for writing the policy. Many of the suggestions are based on two sources: proven best practices for creating library policies and common interlibrary loan policies that have been modified for the small institution.

Creating a Current, Honest, and Accessible Written Policy

In their book on creating policies for libraries, Sandra Nelson and June Garcia list four functions of good policies. First, they help transform an institution's values into action. Second, they give the information they need to perform tasks. Third, policies make sure that "all members of the public know what they can expect from the library and that they are treated equitably" (Nelson and Garcia, 2003: 8). Finally, policies help mitigate legal action against the library. All of these functions must be addressed when developing policy in small interlibrary loan departments.

As mentioned in the introduction to this manual, patrons often think that ILL works like "magic." Policies allow interlibrary loan departments to clearly articulate to patrons both the purpose of the department and the method of processing requests. This is particularly important for small interlibrary loan departments that are often hampered by both budget and staffing constraints. It is often impossible for small departments to provide the same kinds of services as those found in large institutions. Small departments must use policies to set realistic expectations for both staff members and patrons. Policies must have three characteristics to fulfill their functions: they must be current, honest, and accessible.

First, policies must be updated on a regular basis. Technology and procedures can change quickly and it is important for library policies to reflect current practice. As Nelson and Garcia note, there is often a divide between written policy and "how we do business here" (Nelson and Garcia, 2003: 6). When a library does not have updated policies, it leaves itself open to a wide range of problems including charges of unfairness to patrons and threats of copyright infringement. Interlibrary loan policies should be reviewed on an annual basis to ensure that no discrepancies exist between what staff members actually do, what the public thinks staff members do, and what is actually written in the policy.

Second, even though policies are the written embodiment of institutional and professional values, they must also be truthful. If your library will not loan to some types of institutions, it should be clearly stated in the written policy. If your library will not loan certain materials, this information should also be stated in the policy.

Finally, interlibrary loan policies should be easily accessible to anyone who needs information regarding a particular library's services. This means that policies should be posted to the library's Web site, available in hard copy within the physical library building, and, if applicable, uploaded to any cooperating network policy directories. Although widely publicizing policies will not eliminate all inquiries, it will reduce the number that are received and make it easier for staff members to find the answers to questions.

Making Written Policy Match Institutional Practice

It is clear that policies are important, but how should staff members of small ILL departments create one that works for their particular situation? What information should be included in the policy? As mentioned, written policies should match current institutional practice. They should also meet the guidelines stated in the ALA *Interlibrary Loan Code for the United States* (American Library Association, 2008). Although it is true that most library departments want to save both patron and staff time, this is particularly salient to small interlibrary loan departments that usually lack both the personnel and budgets of larger departments.

For small interlibrary loan departments, creating a policy that works might mean that some policy regulations will need to be more stringent than those found in larger libraries. Circumstances in individual libraries might necessitate limiting the kinds of materials that can be lent or the types of institutions that can borrow materials. Thinking these issues through during the policy development process will save time and money in the long run.

Nelson and Garcia's (2003) book on developing library policy, Lee Andrew Hilyer's (2006) book on best practices, and Morris's (2005) article on the interlibrary loan policy offer excellent suggestions for creating good interlibrary loan policies. Their recommendations are discussed throughout this chapter. However, before discussing the process of writing policy, it is important to define the different sections that when combined become what is most commonly thought of as a "policy."

Developing the Policy: Policy Statements, Regulations, Guidelines, and Procedures

The word "policy" is actually an umbrella term for many documents that are used to maintain institutional norms. Most libraries have several of these, including policies for collection development, maintenance of library records, meeting and/or study room use, and, of course interlibrary loan. Policies consist of four different parts: policy statements, regulations, guidelines, and procedures.

Policy statements are similar to mission statements because they describe why the institution provides a particular service. Small interlibrary loan departments should use the departmental mission statement as the policy statement. These statements should reflect the outlook of the library mission statement and describe the overall purpose of the department. The policy statements, regulations, and procedures should flow directly from the departmental mission statement. Lee Andrew Hilyer (2006) notes that mission statements can simply be a list of departmental goals. Remember to have a mission statement before embarking on the process of developing policy as the mission statement will help frame all of the elements of the department's written policy.

Regulations, which define the policy statement, are the core of policy. When most people think of written policies, they are often thinking of regulations. Chapters 6 and 7 discuss specific policy regulations that will help small interlibrary loan departments provide efficient, customer-centered service.

Guidelines, which are philosophical statements based on best practice, are not mandatory (Nelson and Garcia, 2003). Small interlibrary loan departments should not write their own guidelines, but strive to follow the *Interlibrary Loan Code for the United States* (American Library Association, 2008) described in Chapter 4. The policy regulations discussed in Chapters 6 and 7 are based on this code.

Procedures are written, step-by-step instructions for carrying out certain tasks. Writing procedures can be one of the most time-consuming parts of policy writing and, at first glance might not seem to be worth the trouble for small interlibrary loan departments. However, written procedures ensure that anyone on staff can conduct borrowing and lending transactions.

What is commonly called "Interlibrary Loan Policy" actually consists of two different policies: one for borrowing and one for lending. Some might consider the patron policy to be a third type of policy but it is best understood as a version of the borrowing policy written specifically for the library's users. Chapter 6 includes recommendations for borrowing policies and procedures as well as a brief discussion of the patron policy. Lending policies and procedures are discussed in Chapter 7.

Interlibrary loan policies should include a provision for evaluating the services provided by the department. Both quantitative and qualitative measurements should be used to ascertain the quality and consistency of the service. Suggestions for maintaining statistics using basic office software are discussed in Chapter 9. Small departments should pay close attention to their fill rate for both borrowing and lending. This is the number of requests filled divided by the number of requests received then multiplying by 100. A higher fill rate often leads to higher patron satisfaction as patrons are receiving the items they requested.

Patron surveys can be used as a qualitative assessment of the ILL department. Staff members should choose a particular time period (between two weeks and a month) during which each patron is sent a satisfaction survey at the conclusion of their ILL transaction. Online electronic survey services such as Survey Monkey (surveymonkey.com) or Zoomerang (zoomerang.com) are available for free and have greatly reduced the hassle of developing and disseminating surveys to patrons. Small department staff members should use the data from both statistics and surveys to improve overall performance.

Writing the Policy

It is the responsibility of the staff member (or members) who conduct interlibrary loan to write the policy for the department. This person should be familiar with all of the lending and borrowing procedures that are currently in use in the department. In order to make the process as painless as possible, the staff member should complete some preliminary work before actually writing the policy.

First, the staff member should evaluate existing policies and procedures. Some questions to consider include the following: Does your policy include all three elements (policy statements, regulations, and procedures)? (Remember that you do not need guidelines.) Do all of the elements reflect current practice? Are any technological changes accounted for? Members of small interlibrary loan departments should also determine if they can actually meet the expectations of the current policy. Thorough evaluation of the current policy will smooth the updating process.

After the initial evaluation, the staff member should meet with other library personnel that have a stake in the interlibrary loan policy including staff from other departments, administration, and members of the board. Participants in these meetings should discuss changes to the existing policy. Note that other institution's interlibrary loan policies are a valuable resource for writing policy. These are easily found either on the Internet or on OCLC's Interlibrary Loan Policy Directory (https://illpolicies.oclc.org). It is particularly helpful to examine policies used in institutions of similar size and patron base.

Finally, the staff member should write a draft of the new policy. Even if several people (other staff members, management, members of the board) are involved in updating the interlibrary loan policy, only one person should do the actual writing. As Nelson and Garcia clearly state: "Committees do not write, individuals write" (Nelson and Garcia, 2003: 89). The policy should be written for the appropriate audience and should be free of library jargon. After completing the first draft, the committee members should meet to evaluate and modify the draft. The final draft should be sent to the administration for approval.

Small interlibrary loan departments are often in small institutions and it is likely that the "ILL person" will have to do all of the policy revisions alone. In this situation, the staff member should let others know that the policy is in the process of being revised. It is possible that they would be willing to at least look over the drafts if they cannot help in the actual development process.

Format

One of the easiest ways to write a policy is to use a Frequently Asked Questions (FAQs) format. The patron policy, in particular, should be written in this format. This question-and-answer format is familiar to many people from its use on the Internet. It also has the advantage of being easy for staff to update because any additional questions can be easily added to the policy. FAQs should be written in an informal prose style.

Publicizing the Policy: Internal and External Strategies

If the institution has a policy handbook, copies of all of the policies should be included in it. As mentioned in the beginning of this chapter, making policies accessible will reduce the number of inquiries staff members receive about interlibrary loan and help them answer any questions about the policy.

If the library uses WorldCat Resources Sharing (WCRS), information from the lending policy should be included in the OCLC Policies Directory. Fill out the information in the online form as completely as possible using the written lending policy as a guide. Be sure to include as much contact information as possible. It is discouraging to search for an institution's contact person in the directory only to find that there is no way to get in touch with a staff member.

The lending policy should also be posted on the library's Web site. Many institutions do not use WCRS and the Web site is sometimes the easiest way to find out what a particular library's policies are.

The borrowing policy is an internal document that should be available to all department members and administration. The patron policy is the public version of the borrowing policy and should be available on both the library Web site and printed out in hard copy for quick reference within the library.

Confronting Policy Creation Problems in Small Institutions

It is difficult to create good policy. The lack of staff in small institutions can make an already difficult process worse because the burden for developing policy is often placed on one or two people. Staff in small departments might be tempted to overlook some of the steps involved in creating interlibrary loan policy. However, keep in mind that taking the time to develop policy in the present will reduce headaches and frustration in the future.

As lending and borrowing are entirely separate transactions, policies and procedures for each are discussed in separate chapters. Chapter 6 offers specific suggestions for streamlining lending within the small interlibrary loan department. Suggestions for borrowing are in Chapter 7. Both chapters include specific policy statements that can be tailored to an individual library's needs.

References and Works Consulted

American Library Association. 2008. *Interlibrary Loan Code for the United States.* Available: www.ala.org/ala/mgrps/divs/rusa /resources/guidelines/interlibrary.cfm (accessed July 30, 2009).

Brumley, Rebecca. 2006. *The Reference Librarian's Policies, Forms, Guidelines, and Procedures Handbook with CD-ROM.* New York: Neal-Schuman.

Hilyer, Lee Andrew. 2006. *Interlibrary Loan and Document Delivery: Best Practices for Operating and Managing Interlibrary Loan Services in All Libraries.* Binghamton, NY: The Haworth Press.

Morris, Leslie R. 2005. "Why Your Library Should Have an Interlibrary Loan Policy and What Should Be Included." *Journal of Interlibrary Loan, Document Delivery & Electronic Reserve* 15, no. 4: 1–7.

Nelson, Sandra, and June Garcia. 2003. *Creating Policies for Results: From Chaos to Clarity.* Chicago: American Library Association.

Rare Books and Manuscripts Section of the Association of College and Research Libraries. 2004. *Guidelines for the Interlibrary Loan of Rare and Unique Materials.* Available: http://ala.org/ala/mgrps/divs/acrl/standards/rareguidelines.cfm (accessed July 30, 2009).

6

Lending Policies and Procedures Designed to Maximize Staff Resources

This chapter offers recommendations for lending policy regulations and procedures. These recommendations may not work in every institution and should be tailored to a particular department's needs. As many libraries (approximately 7,500) participate in OCLC WorldCat Resource Sharing (WCRS), the suggestions in this chapter assume that departmental staff has access to this bibliographic utility but not to a full-featured interlibrary loan management system (IMS). Chapter 9 discusses some ideas on how to run an interlibrary loan department without using WCRS.

Lending policies and procedures should not be based on fear. A certain nervousness accompanies sending materials through the mail; however, it is important to remember that libraries send books home with patrons. Once an item leaves the library it is out of the library's control whether it is checked out or sent through the mail. It may be a bit more difficult to replace lost items or recoup damage costs when items are sent to borrowing institutions through interlibrary loan, but the burden of this concern should be placed on borrowing libraries, not lending libraries. Remember that the borrowing library is, in essence, simply another patron.

Because small departments must try to fill all local patron requests, it is on the lending side of interlibrary loan that the small department can more easily save staff time and money by streamlining operations and employing simple time management concepts. This chapter helps departments answer the following questions:

- To whom should libraries lend?
- What types of materials should be lent?

- How long should the lending period be?
- When should staff members process lending requests?
- How should these requests be processed?
- Should the institution charge a fee for lending?
- What are some simple ways to keep track of materials and managing workflows?

General Lending Policy Considerations

The interlibrary loan system functions best when all libraries fully participate. This is clearly stated in the national interlibrary code: "The effectiveness of the national interlibrary loan system depends upon participation of libraries of all types and sizes" (American Library Association, 2008: Introduction). However, for many small interlibrary loan departments, it makes sense to craft somewhat restrictive lending policies. This will allow the institution to save both time and money in lending services. Even though the recommendations that follow may seem limiting, both semi-restrictive policies and time-management strategies will help small interlibrary loan departments participate in ILL without allowing the service to overwhelm staff members.

Some of the sections in this chapter include specific policy statements that staff members can modify and use in the library's written ILL policy. These examples are listed in full in Figures 6-1 and 6-2.

Determining Institutional Lending Policies: Develop a Hierarchy

The first question policy regulations should answer concerns which institutions can borrow materials. If resources are available, staff members should try to process all requests, but this is

Figure 6-1: Public Library Lending Policy

**Reading Public Library
Interlibrary Loan Department
Lending Policy**

Contact Information
Reading Public Library
Interlibrary Loan Department
123 Main St.
Anytown, NY 10011–0022
212–123–4567
212–123–4576 (Fax)
illlending@readingpubliclibrary.org
http://www.readingpubliclibrary.org/ill

Who may borrow from the Reading Public Library?
Reading Public Library lends to all institutions within the United States and Canada. We will lend to international libraries outside of Canada on a case-by-case basis.

How do you accept requests?
We accept requests via OCLC ILL (Preferred) and ALA Request Form via e-mail and fax.

What materials will you loan?
Reading Public Library will lend most circulating materials including a/v materials. We do not lend periodicals or books on the New York Times Best Seller List.
• Returnable items are allowed three weeks' use with an option to renew for an additional two weeks.
• We will photocopy noncirculating items.
• Our average turnaround time is three business days.

Do you charge for lending?
Reading Public Library is a reciprocal lender. We charge what you charge! We do not charge members of LVIS and the Metropolitan Library Network. Please note that we only use IFM for billing other libraries.

How do you deliver materials?
Reading Public Library delivers returnable materials via USPS Library Rate and Metropolitan Library Network Courier. Articles are sent via e-mail (preferred) and fax.

Please note that we do not accept "sawdust" Jiffy bags!

Overdue/Damaged/Lost Items
We charge $5 per day for overdue items.

Damaged/Lost items are charged a standard replacement fee of $50/item.

Other Information/Questions
Please contact us directly at the email or telephone number above regarding items from the Genealogy Department.

Reading Public Library Interlibrary Loan Department is closed on New Year's Day, July 4, Labor Day, Thanksgiving Day, and Christmas Day.

Figure 6-2: Academic Library Lending Policy

Reading College
Read Library
Interlibrary Loan Department
Lending Policy

Contact Information
Reading College
Read Library
Interlibrary Loan Department
321 Main St.
Anytown, NY 10011–0022
212–123–4567
212–123–4576 (Fax)
ill@readingcollege.edu
http://library.readingcollege.edu/ill

Who may borrow from Reading College?
Reading College lends to all institutions including those located overseas. Preference is given to libraries in the Metropolitan Library Network.

How do you accept requests?
We accept requests via OCLC ILL (Preferred) e-mail, fax, telephone, and ALA Request Form.

What materials will you loan?
The following materials are available through Interlibrary Loan:
• Circulating books and periodicals
• Microforms
• Maps
• Government Documents
• Photocopies of noncirculating items

Our average turnaround time is two business days.

Do you charge for lending?
Reading College only charges institutions that charge us for borrowing. Please consider becoming a reciprocal lender.

We prefer IFM for billing and charge a $10 processing fee for invoices.

How do you deliver materials?
Reading College delivers returnable materials via USPS Library Rate and Metropolitan Library Network Courier.

We send articles via Odyssey (preferred) and fax.

Overdue/Damaged/Lost Items
We charge $5 per day for overdue items.

Damaged/Lost items are charged a standard replacement fee of $50/item.

Other Information/Questions
Please contact us directly at the email or telephone number above regarding items from our special collections.

Reading College Interlibrary Loan Department operates according to the College's Academic Calendar.

often impossible for small departments that do not have staff dedicated to interlibrary loan. Small ILL departments should try to lend to as many institutions as possible, but should craft policies that will allow staff members to use their time wisely. Even the smallest institution can receive hundreds of requests per year and processing each one can consume vast amounts of staff time.

One of the easiest ways to determine which requests will be processed is to create a hierarchy of institutions based on various characteristics. Institutions that are fellow members of cooperating library networks should always occupy the top level of the hierarchy. Requests from these libraries should always be processed as soon as possible. As mentioned in Chapter 2, participating in these networks can help libraries both control interlibrary loan costs and provide a wider range of range of services to their patrons.

The remaining levels of the hierarchy can be based on other institutional characteristics. Some libraries might choose to always process requests from institutions that are located nearby. Others might process requests from nonprofit institutions before processing those from for-profit organizations. Decisions regarding which institutions can borrow materials should be made in consultation with the library's administration. It is possible that wider organizational considerations must be taken into account when developing the service hierarchy. Morris notes that these decisions do not have to be publicly justified, but all potential borrowers should be able to easily find out if a particular institution will loan them materials (Morris, 2005).

Another important question to consider is whether the library will lend internationally. International interlibrary loan (outside of Canada) is covered by guidelines developed by the International Federation of Library Associations (IFLA). Small interlibrary loan departments should read these guidelines carefully and decide whether they can meet the requirements. Many libraries in the United States will lend to Canada without requiring any special provisions for the service. Lending to Canada is covered by an agreement between the Association of Research Libraries (ARL) and the National Library of Canada. As with the IFLA guidelines, the Canadian guidelines should be read carefully before any policy decisions are made regarding interlibrary loan services with Canadian libraries. Regulations regarding lending to Canadian libraries should be clearly stated in the lending policy.

Receiving Requests

Requests should be received through electronic means. If the department uses WorldCat Resource Sharing, this should be noted as the preferred method for receiving requests in the lending policy regulations. Using one electronic method as much as possible ensures that all requests can be easily retrieved if a problem needs to be addressed. Electronic transmission through WCRS also makes it easier to collect annual statistics.

Even if OCLC is the preferred method, small interlibrary loan departments should accept requests in almost any format, including via fax, e-mail, ALA form, and telephone. If someone on staff has the ability to create an online request form, one should be included on the library's Web site. (Sample forms can be found in Chapter 9.) If a request is received via telephone, staff members should be encouraged to fill out an electronic ALA Request Form (see Figure 6-3) while conducting the interview to ensure that all information is correctly transcribed. All requests, whether they are received electronically or in hard copy, should be marked with the date received. Use spreadsheets (described in Chapter 9) to keep track of requests received outside of WCRS for statistical purposes.

Forms sent via e-mail should be saved in a folder that can be accessed by all departmental staff members. When requests are received via telephone, instead of writing the information in a paper form, fill out the online form or create and send an e-mail to ill@yourinstitution.com. To facilitate this process, consider making a generic request form in a word-processing program that can be easily copied into an e-mail program.

Small departments might want to consider scanning in all lending requests received on paper. These scans should be saved to a

FIGURE 6-3: ALA Interlibrary Loan Request Form 2002

Request date _____
Need before _____
Request number_____
Client information _____

Borrowing library name and address

Citation Information
Book author _____
Book title _____
Publisher _____ Place _____ Date _____
Series _____
This edition only _____ ISBN _____

Serial title _____
Volume / issue _____ Date _____ Pages _____
Author of article _____
Title of article _____
ISSN _____

Audiovisual title _____
Date of publication _____

Verified in and / or cited in _____
Other bibliographic number _____
Lending library name and address

Lending library phone _____
Lending library fax _____
Lending library email _____
Lending library electronic delivery address _____

Notes _____

Request complies with
[ ] 108(g) (2) Guidelines (CCG)
[ ] other provision of copyright law (CCL)

Authorization _____
Phone _____
Fax _____
Email _____
Electronic delivery address _____

Type of request:
[ ] Loan
[ ] Photocopy
[ ] Estimate
[ ] Locations
Charge information
Account number_____
Maximum willing to pay _____
Have reciprocal agreement _____
Payment provided _____
Lending library report
Date of response_____
Date shipped _____
Shipped via _____
Insured for _____
Return Insured [ ]
Packing Requirements _____
Charge _____
Date due_____
Use restrictions
[ ] Library Use Only
[ ] Copying not permitted
[ ] No Renewals
[ ] _____
Not sent because
[ ] At bindery
[ ] Charge exceeds limit
[ ] Hold placed
[ ] In process
[ ] In use
[ ] Lacking
[ ] Lacks copyright compliance
[ ] Locations not found
[ ] Lost
[ ] Non-circulating
[ ] Not found as cited
[ ] Not on shelf
[ ] Not owned
[ ] On order
[ ] On reserve
[ ] Poor condition
[ ] Prepayment required
[ ] Request on _____
[ ] Volume / issue not yet available
[ ] _____
Estimate for
Loan _____
Copy _____
Microfilm _____
Microfiche _____
Borrowing library report
Date Received _____
Date Returned _____
Returned via _____
Insured for _____
Payment Enclosed [ ]
Renewals
Date Requested _____
New Due Date _____
Renewal Denied [ ]

folder that is accessible to all members of the department and is backed up on a regular basis. If it is not possible to scan requests, keep the requests received in a folder in an accessible file drawer. These files should be used as backup for the electronic statistics saved on both WCRS and in a spreadsheet. Staff should maintain these records in accordance with the library's record retention policy.

Policy Statements

- Reading Public Library lends to all institutions within the United States and Canada. We will lend to international libraries outside of Canada on a case-by-case basis. We accept requests via OCLC ILL (Preferred) and ALA Request Form via e-mail and fax.
- Reading College lends to all institutions including those located overseas. Preference is given to libraries in the Metropolitan Library Network. We accept requests via OCLC ILL (Preferred) e-mail, fax, telephone, and ALA Request Form.

Deciding Which Materials Will Be Loaned

Large institutions usually lend almost all of their materials through interlibrary loan including items from special collections, audio/visual materials, and theses and dissertations. Small ILL departments might not have the resources to adequately prepare all of these different types of materials for lending. It is recommended that small ILL departments focus on lending regularly circulating materials and providing copies of periodical articles. Lending materials that can easily survive shipping processes will help the library save money on packaging and shipping costs. Exceptions to this general rule are discussed below. If an institution chooses to lend other types of materials, the parameters for this service should be clearly articulated in the lending policy.

Decisions regarding whether to lend audio/visual materials are often based on the durability of these materials in the past. Records, films, and cassette tapes were often very fragile and expensive and would not survive shipping without using special packaging. Current a/v materials including CDs and DVDs are usually much more robust and should be considered for lending. Rather than restricting a/v materials, it makes more sense for small departments to restrict lending rare and archival materials.

Interlibrary loan of rare materials is governed by guidelines developed by the Rare Books and Manuscripts Section (RBMS) of the Association of College and Research Libraries (ACRL) (2004), a division of ALA. These guidelines "strongly encourage" interlibrary loan from special collections. However, they also note that "the decision to lend <rare> materials should involve the individual exercising curatorial responsibility for those materials" and these decisions "should reflect an item-by-item, series-by-series, or collection-by-collection consideration" (Rare Books and Manuscripts Section, 2004). If a small interlibrary loan department wishes to loan special collections, staff members should be familiar with these guidelines. The lending policy should note that requests will be considered on a case-by-case basis and institutions should contact the person who manages interlibrary loan directly either via e-mail or telephone. Small ILL departments might also want to consider offering fee-based digitizing services for rare and special materials.

Interlibrary loan lending policies for theses and dissertations vary widely across institutions. These items are sometimes difficult for small institutions to loan as there is often only one deposited copy of the work and no easy replacement method it if it is lost. Even though regulations for depositing theses and dissertations are often developed outside of the library, small institutions might want to consider advocating for one of the following guidelines. First, thesis and dissertation deposits should require three copies of the work: one for archival purposes, one for circulation, and one in electronic PDF format. If no space is available for two hard copies, require one for the archive and another in PDF format. These protected PDFs should be placed on a shared file server so that they are easily retrievable and can be borrowed through ILL via e-mail.

If there is only one copy of a thesis or dissertation, small interlibrary loan departments should consider establishing a document delivery service for these items. This means that the institution would charge a processing, copying, and shipping fee for each request. It is recommended that small departments request pre-payment for this service. These requests would be handled on a case-by-case basis. All of this information should be listed in the lending policy. Even though it is tempting to not lend these materials at all, theses and dissertations are often valuable resources for scholars and should be made available through interlibrary loan if at all possible.

Lending policies should also include information regarding whether bound and single issue periodicals will be lent to requesting institutions. In 2007, Steve Lee published a timely article regarding the continuing practice of restrictive journal lending in the age of electronic media. He writes that these limiting policies are unnecessary if the journal title is available in full-text online (Lee, 2007). In general, interlibrary loan departments should follow the circulation policies of the institution. If the library loans bound and single-issue periodicals, so should the interlibrary loan department, especially if the request is for many volumes of material.

If the request is significantly large, it is usually easier for small departments to send microfilm and microfiche to the borrowing library instead of printing out the material in-house. Copying materials in these formats is often extremely time-consuming and it makes sense for small departments to pass this burden on to the borrowing institution. This can also be decided on a case-by-case basis. The staff member can determine if the amount of pages requested is overly burdensome. In any case, the lending policy should state whether the library will lend microforms.

Some libraries do not loan new books for historical reasons (Morris, 2005) but this is an unnecessary restriction that does not meet the national ILL code guidelines. Morris recommends that interlibrary loan staff members develop a matrix of lending availability for all other types of materials including government documents, maps, and slides (Morris, 2005). This information should also be indicated in the lending policy.

Lending Period

The national code states that "the due date is defined as the date the material is due to be checked-in at the supplying library" (American Library Association, 2008). Lending periods for returnable materials should be long enough to allow both shipping and use of the materials. Usually a lending period of between four and six weeks is enough to complete transactions. To keep operations as simple as possible, it is easiest to loan all returnable materials for the same amount of time. If an item is needed before the due date, it should be promptly recalled. Renewals should also be allowed as long as the material is not recalled by a local patron. Information regarding how many renewals are permissible should be included in the lending policy.

Note that the information in this section relates to the due date that is given to the borrowing library. To streamline borrowing operations, the due date in the library's ILS may differ.

Policy Statements

- Reading Public Library will lend most circulating materials including a/v materials. We do not lend periodicals or books on the New York Times Best Seller List. Returnable items are allowed three weeks use with an option to renew for an additional two weeks. We will photocopy non-circulating items.

- Reading College will lend circulating materials including a/v, bound periodicals, microforms, theses, and photocopies of noncirculating materials. Returnable items are allowed four weeks use. Two-week renewals are allowed.
- The following materials are available through Interlibrary Loan:
  - Circulating books and periodicals
  - Microforms
  - Maps
  - Government documents
  - Photocopies of noncirculating items

Developing a Schedule and Setting Time Limits for Processing Requests

Interlibrary loan lending requires a lot of staff time. Processing requests, from receipt to shipment, can require hours of work. When the staff member who conducts interlibrary loan has duties outside of ILL, lending processes should be limited to a set amount of time each week.

There are two methods to accomplish this. First, staff members can process requests on certain days of the week. For example, depending on the number of borrowing requests received, staff members can process requests every Monday, Wednesday, and Friday or every Tuesday and Thursday. Or staff members can process requests every work day, at certain times of the day for a set amount of time. Using either of these solutions means that some requests will be passed along to the next lender in the string. However, there are ways to limit the number of requests that slip through the cracks.

If the department chooses to conduct interlibrary loan on certain days of the week, it is important to check the request queue every day, even if requests are not processed. Large departments usually do not have to complete this step manually because IMSs download and push requests to individual staff members. Staff members of small departments should check the request queue at the same time every day—perhaps at the beginning of the workday or after lunch. Set a reminder task for this activity on personal information software such as Microsoft Outlook. Even though it is tempting to process them as soon as they are received, requests received via e-mail, fax, and postal service should be saved until the next processing day.

WorldCat Resource Sharing keeps requests in the lending queue (see Figure 6-4) for four days. On nonprocessing days, requests should be sent to the next library in the lender string. This ensures that the request will be filled as soon as possible by another library. If the institution is the last library in the string, the request should be saved for the next processing day. Libraries that conduct interlibrary lending on certain days of the work week might choose to save and process requests from cooperating network libraries instead of sending them to the next lender.

Departments that choose to process requests every work day should establish both a set time of day and number of hours to work on lending. Check the request queue either every morning or just after lunch. It might be easier to wait until later in the day to process requests as this will give staff time to complete other tasks earlier in the day. In either case, it is important to work on lending requests for only a certain number of hours. Once that limit is reached, stop processing. The remaining requests can be sent to the next lender or saved for the next day.

Both of these time-management systems have advantages and disadvantages. Processing lending requests on certain days of the week ensures that nonprocessing days can be fully devoted to other tasks. However, it does mean that fewer requests will be processed overall. Allotting a certain number of hours each day to processing requests allows the department to fulfill more requests, but this method might limit the time left for other tasks. Staff members of small library departments must decide which system works better for their situations. Perhaps ILL lending requests are processed on most days except when there is a staff meeting or

Figure 6-4: OCLC WCRS Lending Request Screenshot

Staff View | Display

| Searching | Resource Sharing | | My Account | Options | Policies Directory | Comments | Exit | Hide tips |

Request Manager | Blank Workform | Printing | Batch | My Requests | Go to page ▼

Return Admin LHR Print Help
      Link Update

IN PROCESS - Lender
Record number: 1 Total records: 3

⦿ **Yes**   DEFAULT ▼   ☐ Print Shipping Labels   ☐ Print Book Straps
  Constant Data

○ **No**   In use/on loan ▼
  Reason For No

○ **Conditional** ▼
  Lending Notes

○ **Future Date**   YYYYMMDD 🔟

Update | Reset

◀ 1 ▶
Prev   Next

GENERAL RECORD INFORMATION	
Request Identifier: **53325111**	Status: IN PROCESS 20090424
Request Date: 20090420	Source: ILLiad
OCLC Number: 33205729	
Borrower: **TRN**	Need Before: 20090917
Receive Date:	Renewal Request:
Due Date:	New Due Date:
Lenders: OCL, *OCL, OCL	
Request Type: Copy	

BIBLIOGRAPHIC INFORMATION	
Call Number:	
Uniform Title: Journal of quality management (Greenwich, Conn.)	
Title: Journal of quality management.	
ISSN: 1084-8568	
Imprint: Greenwich, CT : JAI Press, c1996-	
Article: : How to disect a brain do not send PDF	
Volume: 9	
Number: 3	
Date: 2004	
Verified: <TN:274><ODYSSEY:132.174.144.44/ILL> OCLC	

BORROWING INFORMATION	
Patron: Rose Padden Mason, Douglas - Graduate	
Ship To: ILL/Memorial Public Library/123 Main St./City, State 01234	
Bill To: OCLC	
Ship Via: Homing Pigeon	
Electronic Delivery: Odyssey - 132.174.144.44/ILL	
Maximum Cost:	
Copyright Compliance: CCL	
Fax: 614-555-1234	
Email: ill@memorial.lib.org	
Affiliation: LVIS,	
Borrowing Notes: This is a demo record. Do not fill this request.	

LENDING INFORMATION	
Lending Charges:	
Shipped:	
Ship Insurance:	
Lending Notes:	
Lending Restrictions:	
Return To:	
Return Via:	

English | Español | Français | ... | 日本語 | ... | 中文(繁體) | 中文(简体) | Options | Comments | Exit other regular time-intensive activities. Or perhaps requests are processed every day during the school year, but only on certain days of the week during the summer break.

If ILL service is suspended (such as during the winter holidays or spring break for academic libraries) this should be noted in the lending policy (Morris, 2005). As mentioned in Chapter 2, small interlibrary loan departments should strive not to shut down services simply because one staff member is out of the office.

Policy Statements

- Reading Public Library Interlibrary Loan Department is closed on New Year's Day, July 4, Labor Day, Thanksgiving Day, and Christmas Day.
- Reading College Interlibrary Loan Department is closed during Winter Break and Spring Break.

Establishing a Procedure for Processing Interlibrary Loans

As mentioned previously, the procedures in this chapter described tasks typically performed in a small interlibrary loan department that has access to WorldCat Resource Sharing (WCRS) but not to an IMS. It should also be noted that some of the suggestions do not follow all of the recommendations in Boucher's handbook (Boucher, 1997). They do, however, adhere as closely as possible to the guidelines found in the ALA ILL code discussed in Chapter 4 (American Library Association, 2008). Many of the suggestions emphasize ecological awareness and stress methods that save paper.

At the designated time for processing, login to WCRS to check the request queue. Note the number of requests in the queue (see

Figure 6-5). To save time and paper do not print out every request; go through the queue online instead. Keep the queue open while searching the catalog for requested items. Write down call numbers and volume/date information on a piece of paper. If an item is not available, update the queue with a "Reason for No" immediately. If the requested material is available in electronic format, update the request to "Shipped" and send it immediately. Once the staff member has searched the number of requests noted when he or she first logged in, stop searching. Any new requests can be processed the next work day.

After searching in the catalog for the items in the queue, retrieve the materials from the stacks. If items are not found, note this on the piece of paper with the call numbers. It is tempting to spend a lot of time searching for these items, but this task should not be a part of the interlibrary loan process.

The next step is to process items for shipment. First, process all of the returnable materials. Update the request for each one to "Shipped" and mark them "To Be Printed" or print out each request individually as it is updated. This copy will be sent with the item. All materials should be checked out in the library's ILS to a dummy ILL patron. Create either a book strap or a label that lists all of the relevant ILL information including request number, return address, and due date. WCRS can print these automatically but bookstraps and stickers are also easy to create in word processing software.

Boucher recommends that each book be wrapped in craft paper or bubble wrap for shipment (Boucher, 1997), but bubble mailers and boxes that fit snuggly around the books are usually all that is needed to protect most materials. Jiffy mailers (the ones filled with paper dust) are better for the environment but are often a nuisance to open. Do not send them to libraries that do not accept them. It is always nice, but not necessary, to include a return label with the material.

Unless it is specifically requested, returnable materials should be sent Library Rate. Some institutions note in their policies that they prefer First Class mail but sending all returnable materials

Figure 6-5 OCLC WCRS Request Manager Screenshot

Staff View **Request Manager**

Searching   Resource Sharing

Request Manager | Blank Workform | Printing | Batch | My Requests | Go to page ▸

Admin Help
Link

My Account | Options | Policies Directory | Comments | **Exit** | Hide tips

Search Active Requests ⦿
Search Closed Requests ○

Request Identifier (an:) ▸   Search

Borrowing

Action Items	Qty
Recalled	1
Expired	2
Unfilled	2

Work in Progress	Qty
Review	5
Save	1

Information	Qty
Shipped	2
Special Messages/Borrower	11

Lending

Action Items	Qty
In Process	3
Renewal Request	1

Printing

Categories	
Mailing Labels (0 shipping, 0 return)	View	Print
Book Straps (0 Available)		Print

English | Español | Français | عربى | 日本語 | 한국어 | 中文 (繁體) | 中文 (简体) | Options ▸ | Comments | **Exit**

Ⓒ OCLC © 1992-2009 OCLC
Terms & Conditions

Source: Screenshot was taken from OCLC's WorldCat Resource sharing and is used with OCLC's permission. WorldCat® is a registered trademark of OCLC Online Computer Library Center, Inc.

First Class is often too expensive for small departments. If an institution wants the material Rush Delivery, add these costs to the request through IFM. Once materials are returned, remove bookstraps, labels, and paperwork (including thank-you notes). Check the item for damage and then update the request to "Received" in WCRS. Discharge the item from the ILL patron and put it in the proper area for reshelving.

Nonreturnable materials, including article requests, often take more time for small interlibrary loan departments because the department usually lacks a designated scanning and copying person on staff. As discussed in Chapter 9, small departments should try to set up good scanning facilities that can be shared with other departments or with patrons. Scan articles, with a copy of the request as the first page, directly to the responsible staff member's desktop and send the article via e-mail (or ARIEL if available) with the Request ID in the subject line. If scanning services are not available, copy the article and then fax it to the requesting library. If no method of electronic transmission is available, a copy of the article should be sent First Class mail. No matter what method is used, always send the item with a complete copy of the request and update the request to "Shipped."

Program fax machines to generate automatic transmittal notices. If the machine only produces these notices once a week, staff members will not have an immediate way of knowing if the fax was received by the borrowing library. Once a transmission is successful, the original photocopy should be recycled.

Policy Statement

- Reading Public Library delivers returnable materials via USPS Library Rate and Metropolitan Library Network Courier. Articles are sent via e-mail (preferred) and fax.
- Reading College sends articles via Odyssey (preferred) and fax.

Determining Fee Structures and Request Policies

Deciding a fee to charge borrowing libraries can be difficult. Whatever the amount, it should not be arbitrary. There are many different fee structures for charges. For example, some libraries charge a set fee for returnable materials. Others charge a processing fee plus a per page fee for photocopying while others only charge for certain special services. In all circumstances, calculating the charge should be as simple as possible. Most small departments do not receive a lot of requests, so setting up a complicated tiered fee structure does not make much sense.

Another solution might be to charge for lending only when the borrowing library charges for the same service. (This is often indicated in policies with the jaunty phrase "We charge what you charge!") When this method is used, if the borrowing institution charges $20.00 for a book, this is the amount that the lending institution charges for the loan. If another institution does not charge for lending, neither does the supplying library. This can be a somewhat cumbersome solution,as it requires staff members to check the lending policies of each requesting institution. However, in certain circumstances it can encourage libraries to either keep charges low or not charge at all.

As mentioned in Chapter 2, invoicing is often more trouble than it is worth. All small ILL departments should use Interlibrary Loan Fee Management (IFM) if at all possible. If a department has decided not to use invoices, do not send materials to libraries that require invoices. Either send the material without charge or do not send it at all. If libraries cannot participate in IFM, consider establishing electronic methods for collecting payments such as a PayPal account.

Charging for postage was also discussed in Chapter 2. This practice should be eliminated unless the borrowing library requests a special service such as overnight shipping. Morris also notes that libraries should not use coupons. "If you are still selling coupons that are only good for your library, move rapidly to the twenty-first century. No one wants your coupons. Offer to buy back the ones that are out there. Move to IFM" (Morris, 2005: 5).

If a department does not use IFM, staff members should ensure that overdue fees are significant enough to justify sending an invoice. This is also true of any damage and replacement fees. Information regarding all of these fees should be included in the lending policy regulations.

Policy Statement

- Reading Public Library charges what you charge! We do not charge members of LVIS and the Metropolitan Library Network.
- Reading College only charges institutions that charge us for borrowing. Please consider becoming a reciprocal lender.

Management Strategies to Save Time and Resources

As has been mentioned several times, it makes sense for small interlibrary loan departments to save staff time and library resources by employing time management strategies. These strategies include curtailing the amount of time spent looking for items, transmitting information through electronic channels as much as possible, and setting up internal procedures that limit arbitrary busywork.

This section discusses some procedures that can help staff members save time and money when completing lending transactions. As with all of the recommendations in this manual, they should be adapted for particular institutional settings.

ILL Patron

Keeping track of returnable items can be difficult. Some libraries create a separate patron record for each borrowing library but this method is both cumbersome and duplicative. Complete borrowing library information is available through WorldCat Resource Sharing or can be added to electronic and paper request forms.

Instead of creating multiple patrons, small departments should create one ILL patron in the integrated library system. All returnable materials should be checked out to this dummy patron. Using this method makes it easy to see which items are currently charged to borrowing libraries. If a borrowing library needs to be contacted, look up the item in WCRS or in the electronic/hard copy folders. If an item is recalled, change the charge status in the ILS. Overdue and recall notices for the ILL patron should be sent to the ILL department at ill@yourinstitution.com then forward them to the borrowing institution.

Loan Periods and Renewals

Another technique for limiting busywork on the lending side of interlibrary loan is to have a long charge period for the ILL patron. This charge period is for internal use only and is *not* indicated on the request copies that are sent to borrowing libraries. Requests should indicate a borrowing period of between four to six weeks. Long check-out periods of between two to four months for the ILL patron in the ILS helps limit the number of overdue books.

Shipping items Library Rate sometimes takes quite a bit of time. Lengthy loan periods help to mitigate the pressure this shipping time places on the borrowing library. If an item is overdue in the ILS, it has been out of the library for a very long time and any time investigating the loan is entirely warranted.

Renewals by the borrowing library should be allowed as long as the item is not recalled by one of the institution's own patrons.

Check to make sure that the ILL patron charge period covers the requested renewal.

Reasons for No and Conditional Responses

Staff members who conduct interlibrary loan should be familiar with all of the WorldCat Resource Sharing "Reasons for No" and "Conditional" responses. Many of the 17 "Reasons for No" that are currently in use such as "Non Circulating" and "Not Owned," are easy to remember and use, but others are used rarely and often forgotten. These "Reasons for No" can also be used by libraries that are not members of OCLC. They will keep ILL staff from having to reinvent the wheel every time they refuse a request.

Reasons for No

1. In Use/On Loan
2. Non Circulating
3. Not on Shelf/Missing
4. Not Owned
5. Lacking Volume/Issue
6. Branch Policy Problem
7. On Order
8. Cost Exceeds Limit
9. Technical Processing
10. Preferred Delivery Time Not Possible
11. Poor Condition
12. At Bindery
13. Volume Issue Not Yet Available
14. Not Licensed to Fill
15. Required Delivery Services Not Supported
16. Prepayment Required
17. Other

Conditional Responses

1. Not found as cited
2. Duplicate request
3. Borrower concerns/please contact lender
4. Lacks copyright compliance

As noted earlier, departments should create a matrix of all of the different types of material available in the library to determine which will be available for interlibrary loan. The Reason for No "Branch policy problem" should be used if the request is for an item that is not loaned by the institution.

The lending policy procedures suggested previously state that small interlibrary loan departments should not spend a lot of time searching for items that are not easily located on the shelf. Simply use the "Not on Shelf/Missing" Reason for No. Then follow established library procedures for finding missing materials. Hunting for lost books should not be a regular part of interlibrary loan.

When staff members do not have time to process a rush request, use the "Preferred Delivery Time Not Possible" reason.

If an institution prefers not to send items via First Class mail or commercial shipping, they should use the "Required Delivery Services Not Supported" reason. Large institutions often have regular pickups from UPS and FedEx as well as extensive mailing facilities. Small institutions usually have to call for a pick up from a commercial service or walk packages to the local post office to send them overnight. It is acceptable not to fulfill a request to avoid using expensive and time-intensive shipping methods.

"Prepayment Required" should be used judiciously. If the request is for an item that should be filled using document delivery services, mark the request as "Conditional" not "Prepayment Required," as the latter will send the request to the next lender in the string. "Prepayment Required" should not be used for borrowing institutions that prefer an invoice. Use "Conditional" to inform them that only IFM can be used for payment. Avoid using "Prepayment Required" except under special circumstances.

WCRS has established very specific guidelines for using the "Conditional" response. "Conditional" means that the item will be supplied if certain stipulations are met. The system is automatically reset to give the borrowing library four days to respond. Using a Conditional response *requires* a lending note that explains the terms borrowing libraries need to fulfill in order to receive the item. OCLC recommends using Conditional for several conditions including copyright compliance, payment issues, inadequate address information, and if the supplier needs to contact the borrower directly (OCLC, 2008).

Since July 2008, WCRS provides four system-generated lending notes. These are "Not found as cited," "Duplicate request," "Borrower concerns," and "Lacks copyright" (OCLC, 2008). Other lending notes can be created in the system's Administrative Module. Small lending libraries should have a note that states "Lender prefers IFM." Use this lending note whenever a requesting institution asks for an invoice.

Bookstraps and Labels

Lending libraries can decide whether or not to bookstrap or label materials (see Chapter 9 for templates). If creating these items takes too much time, do not make them and send returnable materials with the updated request form. Many libraries will create their own identifying labels for borrowed books after they are received.

Bookstraps and labels have both benefits and drawbacks. Bookstraps do not damage materials but take more time to attach to books. They are also more likely to fall off when the patron is using the item. Labels are easy to use but many librarians will not use them because of preservation concerns as the glue used in removable labels might damage materials.

As mentioned previously, it is nice gesture if the lending library includes a return label. Create a batch of labels in a word processing program and cut them to the correct size so they are easy to add to the shipping package. It is not necessary (though it is preferred) to print labels on preprinted label sheets. Labels (both return and shipping) can also be printed on plain paper and cut to the correct size. Either label can be taped to mailing packages.

Packaging

In her handbook on interlibrary loan, Boucher writes that "the best way to ship books is to wrap the volume in bubble wrap or brown paper and put it in a sturdy cardboard carton or cardboard book mailer. Not every library can afford to do this" (Boucher, 1997: 60). Most small departments fit into this category. It does not make much sense to wrap materials in bubble wrap just to place them in a bubble or jiffy mailer. Boucher also notes that tape, never staples, should be used to close packages (Boucher, 1997).

To save money, interlibrary loan departments should save the small book boxes that are received in the acquisitions department. These boxes are often the perfect size for sending individual books in the mail. If the library still orders microfilm, staff members should save a few of the mailing boxes for shipping.

Deciding which type of mailers to use can be controversial. Jiffy mailers are more ecologically sound but can be quite annoying to open. Bubble mailers are not recyclable but are easier to use. If the library does not have to go through institutional purchasing, check the Internet for the best price. No matter what kind of mailer the department uses, staff members should reuse any mailers that are received by the department that are still in good condition.

Items from special collections should be packaged according to the RBMS Guidelines (Rare Books and Manuscripts Section, 2004).

Shipping Rates

Staff members of small departments should be familiar with the U.S. Postal Service (USPS) shipping rates. The differences between the shipping rates are arcane but departments can save money over time if the correct shipping method is used consistently. Note that shipping regulations change frequently and staff members should be aware of any adjustments to package service rates.

Boucher offers an average book weight of two pounds. "The cost per book will be the charge for the first pound, the cost for one additional pound, and the packaging material" (Boucher, 1997: 61). This information can be used for budgeting purposes.

Almost all materials should be sent Library Rate. This is a specially negotiated rate for libraries, museums, and other nonprofit organizations. As of the end of 2008, the library rate is 7 cents cheaper than "Media Mail" and 11 cents cheaper than "Bound Printed Matter."

Almost all library materials can be sent library rate, including books, a/v materials, and microforms up to 70 pounds. The rate does not require a special permit and all packages should be marked "Library Mail" and "Presorted." Shipping via library rate takes between 2 and 9 days.

Photocopies, which are usually much lighter than books, should be sent First Class mail. Small departments should only send photocopies through the mail if the borrowing library does not accept e-mails or faxes. If the borrowing request does not include an e-mail address or fax number, check the institution's Web site. If this information is not listed on the Web site, give the interlibrary loan department a call. It is worth extra minutes of work to contact the institution in order to save money on postage and enable the patron to receive the requested item more quickly.

Overdue and Recalled Materials

If an ILL patron with a long charge period is set up in the IMS, there will be fewer overdue materials. All overdue notices should be directed to the ILL department at ill@yourinstitution.com. If an overdue notice is generated, check the shelves to make sure that the item was not returned to the stacks without being checked in.

If the item is not on the shelf, forward the overdue notice to the borrowing institution. Put the request ID number in the Subject

Line with the word Overdue. If no response is received within a reasonable time (around 5 business days), call the borrowing staff at the institution. Be sure to have the request ID number on hand when calling.

As the checkout time is so long, departments should charge a fee for overdue ILL books. These fees should be indicated on the overdue notice. If the book is returned without payment for the overdue fee, it often makes more sense to remove the charge instead of trying to follow up with the borrowing institution. Even though it is tempting to do so, there is no reason to be punitive with ILL fees, particularly if the institution has already been charged for borrowing the item. Focus on getting the materials back to the library. If a particular institution is often overdue, call the requesting library's borrowing department to find out if there are any mitigating circumstances.

If materials are not returned, borrowing libraries should be charged regular replacement fees. Replacement costs are often significant and therefore it makes sense to send an invoice and follow up on these fees.

When an item charged out through interlibrary loan is needed by a local patron, it should be recalled through WorldCat Resource Sharing and in the ILS as soon as possible. Interlibrary loan departments often give a short grace period for returning the item and then charge daily overdue fees. Some institutions do not bother recalling materials and instead try to retrieve the item through interlibrary loan.

Damaged Materials

Receiving damaged materials through interlibrary loan is disheartening. Although many ILL departments are particularly sensitive to materials damaged by the shipping process, materials can also be damaged by the requesting patron. The author's library once lent a brand new book through interlibrary loan and it was returned with writing and highlighting on every page.

In these situations, small departments should call the borrowing department of the requesting library. Staff members should know how the materials were damaged and what the replacement cost will be. This phone call should be followed by an e-mail with an electronic invoice attached.

Other Lending Considerations

Lending policies should include the average turnaround time for requests. This is defined as the "number of days from the receipt of a request until the shipment of the item" not including mailing time (Morris, 2005: 3). It is helpful for borrowing institutions to know how long it will take to receive requested items.

Complete contact information for the interlibrary loan department should also be included in the policy. This includes the name of the person who conducts interlibrary loan, a phone number, a fax number, ARIEL address if it is used, and an e-mail address. The e-mail address for the department should be ill@ yourinstitution.com in order to ensure continuity when there is staff turnover (Morris, 2005: 3). Mailing addresses should be as complete as possible including the zip code + 4. If the institution uses a P.O. Box for most interlibrary loan packages, a street address should be given for commercial shipping providers such as FedEx and UPS.

Streamlining Lending Procedures

In all aspects of interlibrary lending, small departments should discard unneeded processes. There is no reason to save paperwork if complete borrowing information is saved electronically. Use WorldCat Resource Sharing as much as possible to maintain historical records instead of keeping paper copies of each request. Small departments should attempt to run a paperless office.

Do not waste time when processing requests. If the material is not easily found or shipped, do not fulfill the request. Send the request to the next lender in the string. Carefully wrapping $15.00 paperbacks to put them in bubble mailers can take a lot of staff time. Save valuable packaging materials for more valuable items.

Finally, conduct interlibrary lending with as much generosity as possible. In the past, policies and procedures were sometimes created in an atmosphere of fear, as if sending books through the mail was significantly worse than sending them home with patrons. The entire interlibrary loan system is based on the idea that libraries will treat other institution's materials as their own. It is important to remember that once materials are outside of the library, librarians no longer have any control over them whether they are at home with patrons or sent to other institutions.

References

American Library Association. 2008. *Interlibrary Loan Code for the United States.* Available: www.ala.org/ala/mgrps/divs/rusa/resources/guidelines/interlibrary.cfm (accessed July 30, 2009).

Boucher, Virginia. 1997. *Interlibrary Loan Practices Handbook.* Chicago: American Library Association.

Lee, Steve. 2007. "In 2007 Should We Be Loaning Journals?" *SCONUL Focus* 41: 37–39.

Morris, Leslie R. 2005. "Why Your Library Should Have an Interlibrary Loan Policy and What Should Be Included." *Journal of Interlibrary Loan, Document Delivery & Electronic Reserve* 4: 1–7.

OCLC. 2008. *WorldCat Resource Sharing Documentation.* Dublin, OH: OCLC. Available: www.oclc.org/us/en/support/documentation/resourcesharing/ (accessed July 30, 2009).

Rare Books and Manuscripts Section of the Association of College and Research Libraries. 2004. *Guidelines for the Interlibrary Loan of Rare and Unique Materials.* Available: http://ala.org/ala/mgrps/divs/acrl/standards/rareguidelines.cfm (accessed July 30, 2009).

Borrowing Policies and Procedures Designed to Maximize Staff Resources

The ALA ILL code notes that "In the interest of providing quality service, libraries have an obligation to obtain material to meet the informational needs of users when local resources do not meet those needs. Interlibrary loan (ILL), a mechanism for obtaining material, is essential to the vitality of all libraries" (American Library Association, 2008: Introduction). These statements are particularly true of small institutions, which often have collections that match their size. Small libraries must use interlibrary loan to supplement their local collections. Budget and staff constraints make it difficult for small institutions to employ all of the technological advancements that have greatly improved interlibrary loan service in large institutions. However, even small libraries should allow patrons to borrow the materials they need and want through interlibrary loan. Unfortunately, it is tempting for small departments to limit ILL borrowing due to concerns about overwhelming staff and exhausting finances.

The borrowing policy and procedures suggestions that follow will help small departments provide excellent borrowing service for patrons without overwhelming staff and resources. This chapter answers the following questions:

- Who can borrow through ILL?
- What materials can be borrowed?
- When should staff members process borrowing requests?
- How should these requests be processed?
- Should patrons be charged for ILL?
- What are some ways to streamline borrowing workflows?

General Borrowing Policy Considerations

To adhere to the ILL code for the United States, small departments should exercise caution when limiting borrowing. Instead of limiting borrowing for patrons, small departments should consider limiting lending to other libraries using the strategies described previously. This allows libraries to provide their own patrons with the best service possible. Staff members should complete borrowing requests before lending requests. Remember that all lending requests do not have to be filled because other libraries, with the same material and more people on staff, can also fill the request.

As in the previous chapter, the suggestions in this chapter are general and should be tailored to an individual institution's needs. Some of the sections include specific policy statement examples. (See Figures 7-1 and 7-2 for complete examples of borrowing policies.) It is assumed that staff members have access to OCLC's WorldCat Resource Sharing (WCRS) but not to a full-featured interlibrary loan management system (IMS).

Maximizing Borrowing Services

Small interlibrary loan departments should allow as many library card holders as possible to use ILL borrowing services. Although some restrictions on who may use the policy make sense (alumni are no longer paying tuition, so they should not receive the same services), borrowing limits should not be implemented arbitrarily. If the current borrowing library policy includes limits on the patron types who may use borrowing services for what may seem like arbitrary reasons, libraries might consider lifting the restriction to evaluate whether an unlimited borrowing policy over-

Figure 7-1: Public Library Borrowing Policy

Reading Public Library
Interlibrary Loan Department
Borrowing Policy

Contact Information
Reading Public Library
Interlibrary Loan Department
123 Main St.
Anytown, NY 10011–0022
212–123–4567
212–123–4576 (Fax)
illborrowing@readingpubliclibrary.org
http://www.readingpubliclibrary.org/ill

What is the purpose of Interlibrary Loan?
Through a process of borrowing items from other libraries, interlibrary loan expands the range of materials available to our patrons.

Who can use ILL?
All library patrons in good standing possessing a valid library card may borrow through interlibrary loan.

What can I borrow?
We will try to borrow whatever you request. Some materials are more difficult to borrow, including current bestsellers and some CDs and DVDs.

We will not borrow items owned by the library. Please recall an item through our catalog if it is currently checked out.

Does it cost anything to borrow materials?
Reading Public Library charges $5 for each requested item. Fees are collected when the material is picked up at the circulation desk.

How do I request an item?
Please place requests using the following forms:
Books
Articles

Where do I pick up my materials?
Articles will be e-mailed to you. The processing fee will be added to your account.

Other materials can be picked up at the circulation desk.

How long can I keep my items?
The due dates for items are set by the lending library. Please return materials to the circulation desk by the date indicated on the bookstrap.
- Overdue items will be charged $1 per day.
- Damaged/Lost items are charged a standard replacement fee of $50/item.

Other Information/Questions
Please contact us directly at the e-mail or telephone number above if you have any questions.

Reading Public Library Interlibrary Loan Department is closed on New Year's Day, July 4, Labor Day, Thanksgiving Day, and Christmas Day.

Figure 7-2: Academic Library Borrowing Policy

Reading College
Read Library
Interlibrary Loan Department
Borrowing Policy

Contact Information
  Reading College
  Read Library
  Interlibrary Loan Department
  321 Main St.
  Anytown, NY 10011–0022
  212–123–4567
  212–123–4576 (Fax)
  ill@readingcollege.edu
  http://library.readingcollege.edu/ill

The mission of the Reading College/Read Library Interlibrary Loan department is to support the academic objectives of the College by expanding the range of materials available to students, faculty, and staff beyond those available through Read Library.

Who can use ILL?
Interlibrary loan services are available to all faculty staff, and currently enrolled students. Alumni may use the service for an additional $10 fee for each item.

What can I borrow?
We will try to borrow whatever you request. Some materials are more difficult to borrow, including bound periodicals and theses and dissertations.

We will not borrow materials available at the Reading State University. Reading College affiliates have full borrowing privileges at Reading State and must obtain these materials on their own.

Does it cost anything to borrow materials?
Reading College absorbs up to $20 of borrowing fees. If the lending library charges more than this amount, library staff will contact the patron.

How do I request an item?
If you are using one of the databases in FirstSearch, simply click "ILL" icon, and fill out the patron information in the request form.

If you are using our catalog or another set of databases, please place requests using the following forms:
  Books
  Articles
Please fill out all forms as completely as possible.

Where do I pick up my materials?
Articles will be e-mailed to you. Other materials can be picked up at the circulation desk.

(continued)

(continued)

How long can I keep my items?
The due dates for items are set by the lending library. Please return materials to the circulation desk by the date indicated on the bookstrap.

- Overdue items will be charged $5 per day.
- Damaged/Lost items are charged a standard replacement fee of $50/item.

Other Information/Questions
Please contact us directly at the e-mail or telephone number above if you have any questions.

Reading College Interlibrary Loan Department operates according to the College's Academic Calendar.

---

whelms institutional resources. As Virginia Boucher notes in her handbook on interlibrary loan, denying services "may dampen rather than foster the pursuit of knowledge" (Boucher, 1997: 4).

Instead of limiting who can borrow, small departments may want to limit the number of requests that can be received at any one time. One strategy to use to assign limits on patron groups in an equitable manner is to list all patron types and then group them according to primary or secondary (or even tertiary if necessary) patron groups. ILL borrowing privileges can then be allocated according to these groupings. At least two questions need to be addressed if a library chooses to limit requests. First, does the limit include both open and pending requests? Second, do all patron types receive the same limit? These limitations should be clearly articulated in the borrowing and patron policy regulations.

Although limitations on borrowing can reduce the amount of work for staff members in some circumstances, they can also increase staff members' workloads as they have to make sure that the limits are enforced. Perhaps, instead of limiting who can borrow, small departments should consider limiting which types of materials can be borrowed. If staff can manage the current number of requests for borrowing, do not impose limits. Some patrons might try to abuse the service but these individuals should be handled on a case-by-case basis if at all possible.

Policy Statements

- All library patrons in good standing and possessing a valid library card may borrow through interlibrary loan.
- All faculty, staff and currently enrolled students may borrow materials through ILL. Alumni are ineligible for this service.
- Interlibrary loan services are available to all faculty staff, and currently enrolled students. Alumni may use the service for an additional $10.00 fee for each item.

Borrowing Directly from Reciprocal Libraries

Instead of limiting the number of borrowing requests a patron can make, small interlibrary loan departments should not borrow any materials that are readily available from institutions with reciprocal borrowing agreements. Encourage patrons to use all of the bibliographic resources available in the area. Even though some of these agreements include provisions for shuttling borrowed materials between libraries, many do not. In the latter case, patrons should be required to visit the cooperating library and check out the materials themselves when they are available. Cooperating library networks can help reduce service burdens placed on any one ILL department, particularly agreements that allow reciprocal borrowing privileges.

This can be an extraordinarily difficult policy regulation to enforce. Patrons usually prefer that materials come to them rather than the other way around. Expect many complaints. Staff members should use the written patron policies to help explain how this regulation keeps institutional costs for interlibrary loan as low as possible. The policy should point out that it is often faster for patrons to pick up items themselves rather than borrow them through interlibrary loan. Front-line staff should be fully versed in this policy and have ready answers to any questions/complaints they might receive. If this policy regulation is impossible to implement, library administrators should try to ensure that consortial and reciprocal agreements allow free or low-cost interlibrary loan between member institutions.

As mentioned, interlibrary loan departments should not limit borrowing requests by type of material. The limit on materials does not refer to format; patrons should be able to borrow anything that another library is willing to lend. Depending on the type of library, patrons might work on projects that require access to special materials. Staff members should contact patrons to find out more information regarding requests for unusual materials. For example, if a patron needs to borrow theses or dissertations, staff members might want to conduct a thorough interlibrary loan interview with the patron. It is possible that these materials will only be available through a document delivery service, which would lead to substantial transaction costs. These extra costs are usually passed on to the patron and he or she should be fully aware of this policy before the request is put through.

Policy Statements

- Reading Public Library will not borrow materials owned by any branch of the library.
- Reading College will not borrow materials available at the Reading State University. Reading College affiliates have full borrowing privileges at Reading State and must obtain these materials on their own.
- "Because the National Judicial College Library, Truckee Meadows Community College Library, the Desert Research Institute Library, and the Washoe County Library are geographically close to the university, materials located at those libraries are not eligible to be requested through interlibrary loan" (Brumley, 2006: 179).

Developing and Maintaining a Borrowing Request Schedule

The borrowing request queue should be checked every working day. Without an IMS, staff members must remember to log into WCRS every day to see if requests are pending. The easiest way to do this is to check the borrowing queue at the same time as the lending queue—either at the beginning of the work day or just after lunch. Set a task on personal information software, such as Microsoft Outlook, as a reminder. The number of borrowing requests that need to be processed might have an effect on the number of lending requests that can be filled.

The previous chapter discussed two time management systems that can be used to handle lending requests: processing requests on certain days or processing requests for a certain length of time each day. Unfortunately, these systems do not work as well for borrowing requests because departments cannot predict how many requests they will have on any given day. For example, academic library departments often have fewer requests during the summer, so department staff might have more time to complete lending requests. Small departments must determine the balance between borrowing and lending that works for their individual situation.

If the number of requests from patrons is overwhelming, small departments can also lessen the burden of processing by using user-initiated borrowing. This method, described in Chapter 2, has been proven to lessen costs and provide more timely service for patrons. WCRS has two methods for setting up user-initiated borrowing: one which sends requests directly to lenders and another which sends requests either to lenders or to the review file, depending on the profile. Small departments that receive a large number of borrowing requests must take the time to establish profiles for user-initiated borrowing.

Providing borrowing services also points to the importance of cross-training in interlibrary loan. Because borrowing services should be available whenever the library is open, it is necessary to ensure that other staff can cover the department when the ILL person is on leave.

Policy Statements

- Reading Public Library Interlibrary Loan Department is closed on New Year's Day, July 4, Labor Day, Thanksgiving Day, and Christmas Day.
- Reading College Interlibrary Loan Department operates according to the Academic Calendar.

Establishing Staff Procedures for ILL Borrowing

As mentioned previously, the following suggestions for procedures assume that staff members have access to WorldCat Resource Sharing but not to an IMS. Some of the procedural suggestions will not apply for user-initiated borrowing practices. As in the previous chapter, some of the suggestions do not follow Boucher's (1997) recommendations but they do adhere closely to the national ILL code (American Library Association, 2008). Many ideas also stress being ecologically sound by saving paper.

Requests for materials that need to be borrowed through interlibrary loan sometimes begin at the reference desk. Reference desk staff should be fully apprised of interlibrary loan policy and procedures in order to provide patrons with accurate and timely service. Small institutions should encourage reference staff to think of themselves as the first line of customer service within the interlibrary loan department.

Patrons who are working on sizeable projects should receive more in-depth information regarding the procedures of interlibrary loan. For example, if a patron needs many items, he or she should not request them all at one time. Processing a few requests at a time will give the patron adequate time to use all of the material. Library staff should be prepared to explain this practice to patrons.

Knowledgeable staff is particularly important at institutions that do not loan books available at other libraries with reciprocal borrowing privileges. They must encourage patrons to visit another library and retrieve the materials themselves. To facilitate this process, reference staff should have ready answers for patrons who question this policy as well as complete directions to the other library.

Staff should also be familiar with the institution's electronic request methods. Although small departments should accept paper requests from patrons as a method of last resort, these should not be used by reference desk staff members. Staff members should always use electronic request forms.

After logging into WCRS, interlibrary loan staff should check the borrowing request review file (see Figure 7-3). To save time and paper, do not print out the requests. All processing functions should be conducted online.

One of the most time-consuming aspects of interlibrary loan involves finding appropriate suppliers. One way to simplify this process is employ efficient use of OCLC's network borrowing symbols. Interlibrary loan staff members should have a hard copy chart of all different cooperating networks to which the institution belongs (see Figure 7-4).

The chart should include both the network symbol and a brief description of the agreement between libraries. For example, a library in a medium-sized city might be part of a geographical network that provides free photocopies and courier service for returnable items. This network, along with brief information regarding fees for supplying materials, should be listed in the chart. Individual institutions that are frequent suppliers but not members of cooperating networks should also be listed. Policies for most lending libraries are listed in the OCLC ILL Policy Directory,

Figure 7-3: OCLC WCRS Request Manager Screenshot

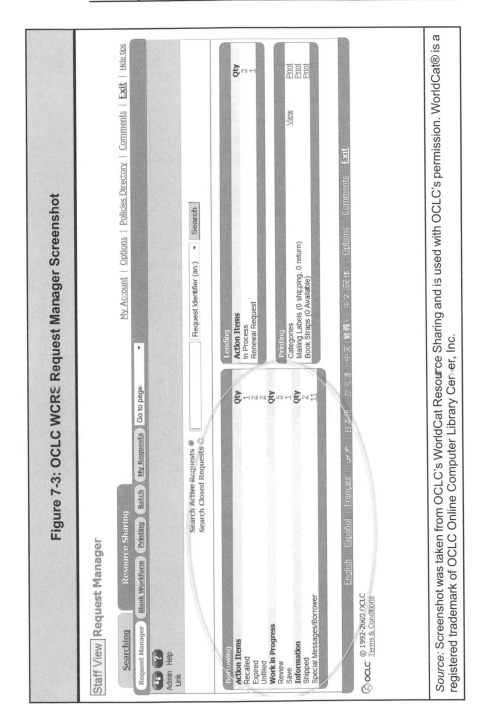

Source: Screenshot was taken from OCLC's WorldCat Resource Sharing and is used with OCLC's permission. WorldCat® is a registered trademark of OCLC Online Computer Library Center, Inc.

Figure 7-4: Library Network Chart		
Network Symbol	**Network Name**	**Services**
MLN	Metro. Library Network	Free copies, courier
MPQ	State Library Network	Courier

which is available either online through WCRS or book form. Most libraries also post their lending policies on their Web sites.

When searching for a supplying library, the networks and libraries on this chart should be searched first according to several factors including the type of material requested, the level of service agreement, and the location of the potential supplying library. Over time, staff members will become more familiar with the lending policies of the networks and libraries listed on the chart. Boucher notes that "the best choice is to pick a library close to you that will give you quick and inexpensive service" (Boucher, 1997: 37).

Now that OCLC's union catalog is available at WorldCat.org, it is easier for libraries without access to bibliographic utilities to find supplying libraries. Small departments should create a user profile on the site to which all members of the department have access and add cooperating network member libraries to the "Favorite Libraries" list (see Figure 7-5). This will push these libraries to the top whenever a search is performed.

Once supplying institutions are identified, the entire lender string should be filled to avoid resending requests. OCLC charges a fee for every request sent through its system whether filled or not. Unnecessary fees should be avoided as much as possible. Try to distribute requests among several different libraries; go to the bottom of the list of suppliers and pick in reverse alphabetical order or choose from the middle of the list.

If the library is connected to systems such as DOCLINE for medical libraries or a local catalog for certain library networks, this system should be used first. If the library does not use these al-

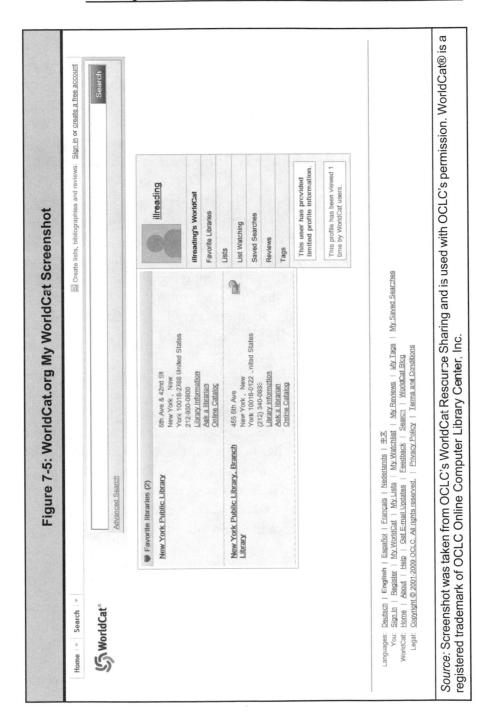

Figure 7-5: WorldCat.org My WorldCat Screenshot

Source: Screenshot was taken from OCLC's WorldCat Resource Sharing and is used with OCLC's permission. WorldCat® is a registered trademark of OCLC Online Computer Library Center, Inc.

ternative systems, staff members with access to WCRS should send all requests through OCLC's system. If a request was originally received on paper or through e-mail, key the information into an online form. Libraries without access to WCRS should send ALA forms as these are accepted by almost all libraries. Use the writable PDF version on the ALA Web site and send the form via e-mail to a supplying library. If the request is for a photocopy, note whether it conforms to CGL (CONTU Guidelines) or CCL (Copyright Law). A copy of this form should also be saved to a folder that is accessible to all members of the department. If forms are received from unverified sources, either on paper or through an electronic form that patrons must key in, requests should be verified before they are sent to supplying libraries. Boucher's (1997) handbook notes that libraries must have well-designed forms if they use unmediated interlibrary loan. One advantage of electronic forms is that HTML can be used to require patrons to fill out necessary fields for complete citations (see Figure 7-6; required fields are starred). Verification of citations is discussed in depth in the following.

The national ILL code states that the requesting library assumes "responsibility for borrowed material from the time it leaves the supplying library until it has been returned to and received by the supplying library" (American Library Association, 2008: 4.8). If an item is lost in the mail before it is received, it is the borrowing library's responsibility to replace it. The same is true if the supplying library does not receive the item after it is returned by the borrowing library.

Once returnable items are received, carefully remove them from their packaging, saving any material that can be reused. Update the request to "Received." If the materials do not have a bookstrap or label, create one in either WCRS or a word processing program. Remember that labels are somewhat controversial and should not be placed on materials from libraries that specifically ask that they not be used. If there is already a visual, cue on the material, do not create a new one. Simply add any local infor-

Figure 7-6: OCLC WCRS Borrowing Form Screenshot

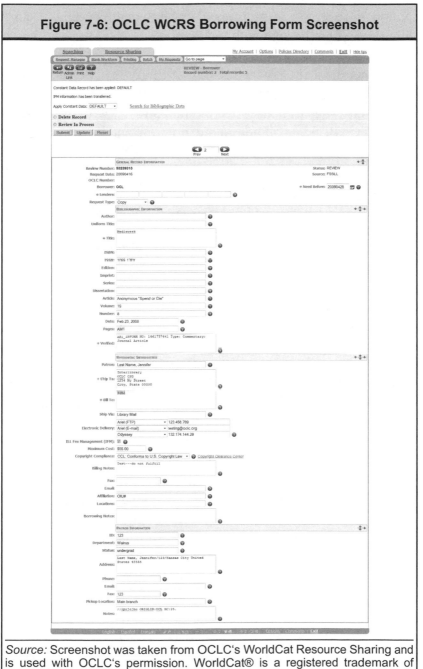

Source: Screenshot was taken from OCLC's WorldCat Resource Sharing and is used with OCLC's permission. WorldCat® is a registered trademark of OCLC Online Computer Library Center, Inc.

mation and note use restrictions on the bookstrap or label. Return labels can either be kept with the item or saved by the staff member in a folder.

Another difficult task for small interlibrary loan departments is figuring out how to keep track of returnable materials. The IMS used by large departments often interact directly with the library's ILS. They will create bibliographic, holding, and item records that can be used to check the item out to the patron and then delete the record in a timely manner. This application is difficult for small departments to replicate. Some libraries key in short records for ILL materials using a method that is similar to an IMS. Others simply keep a list of all of the items that are currently out on loan in a spreadsheet. Small departments must choose which method works best.

If the department chooses to create a spreadsheet, identifying information must be deleted once an item is returned. Libraries using this method must be sure to add each item to the file and check it on a regular basis to notify patrons of any problems. This method is described more fully in Chapter 9.

Setting interlibrary loan due dates is somewhat tricky. The national ILL code defines due dates as "the date the material is due to be checked-in at the supplying library" (American Library Association, 2008: 4.10). Therefore, the patron must return the material to the borrowing library by a date that allows for shipping time. Shipping materials via Library Rate generally requires between two and nine days, so set the patron's due date between one week and ten days before the lending library's due date. Boucher observes that "it is difficult for a patron to finish with borrowed materials in less than two weeks" (Boucher, 1997: 47). If the supplying institution's due date does not allow adequate use, request a renewal while checking in materials.

Patrons should be notified of the availability of materials via e-mail whenever possible. It is usually easiest if patrons pick up materials at the circulation desk. The e-mail should include information regarding pickup location and the due date. If the patron does not have an e-mail address, notify the individual by telephone. Avoid mailing notices.

If dummy item records are added to patron's records, these should be updated when a book is recalled. Otherwise, notify the patron of overdue and recalled materials via e-mail. If possible, add any accumulated overdue fees to the patron's ILS record even if the department does not use dummy records to track ILL.

Circulation desks should have a designated area for returned interlibrary loan materials to ensure they are not sent to the library's stacks. Once materials are returned by the patron, the request should be updated to "Returned" in WCRS. Any tracking information, either in the ILS or in spreadsheet, should be deleted. (Statistical information is kept in a separate chart.) Borrowed materials should be packaged in the manner requested by the supplying library. Mail materials Library Rate using either labels supplied by the lending institution or labels created in either WCRS or a word processing program.

Small interlibrary loan departments should try to receive all photocopies via electronic means if at all possible. Atlas Systems has offered their Odyssey document delivery system free of charge since 2005. Another option is to use Infotreive's ARIEL system which offers both a full featured and receive-only application. These systems should be used if an institution has the means to do so.

If departments do not have access to these systems, borrowing requests on WCRS should include constant data that encourage supplying libraries to send photocopies via e-mail (to ill@ yourinstitution.com) or by fax. When requests are received by either of these methods, remember to update the request to "Received." Article and journal titles should be entered into a spreadsheet to comply with copyright law. More information regarding this method for managing copyright is discussed below.

Items received via e-mail should be forwarded to the patron's e-mail address. Faxes and items received through the mail can be held at the circulation desk. Either send an e-mail or call patrons to notify them that the material is available. If the department has sufficient time and the facilities to do so, these items can be scanned in and sent to patrons as e-mail attachments.

Policy Statements

- Materials can be picked up at the circulation desk.
- Article requests will be delivered via e-mail.
- Please do not return materials in the drop box. Return them to the circulation desk.

Avoiding Borrowing Fees

Charging borrowing fees to patrons for borrowing is a controversial issue (Hilyer, 2002). Patrons usually do not want to pay fees and libraries prefer not to charge them. However, interlibrary loan is not free and libraries often need to recoup their costs. It is often financially impossible for small interlibrary loan departments not to charge borrowing fees to patrons because budget constraints simply do not allow free service. However, if at all possible small interlibrary loan departments should consider not charging fees to patrons. Collecting fees from patrons can take significant staff time and the fees that are charged often do not cover the costs of the borrowing transaction.

In his book on managing ILL in large academic libraries, Lee Andrew Hilyer writes that administrators should "conduct a basic ILL cost analysis and charge only the minimum amount necessary to recover costs" (Hilyer, 2002: 30). This is also a good policy for small interlibrary loan departments. Any fees that are charged to patrons should make financial sense. Some libraries charge fees to discourage patrons from making too many requests (Hilyer, 2002: 30) but other methods that do not punish all users can be used to discourage patrons from making too many requests.

If an institution does decide to charge borrowing fees, these should be explicitly stated in the borrowing policy regulations.

Departments can use several strategies for charging fees. For example, some libraries state that the institution will cover all borrowing costs up to a certain amount. Patrons must cover the fee after this maximum charge is met. Another solution might be to charge fees for all borrowing requests whether or not the actual transaction incurs a fee from the supplying library. Information regarding how fees are collected should also be included in the borrowing policy.

Most libraries collect money at circulation desks for overdue and lost book fees; therefore, fees for interlibrary loan should be collected in the same location. If it is important for these fees to remain in separate revenue stream, train circulation workers to collect different fees using a method that easily identifies which monies are for which types of charges. Perhaps circulation fees can be collected in one envelope and interlibrary loan fees in another. To facilitate collection, create fee slips in a word processing program that can be easily attached to the material.

Unfortunately, collecting money for photocopies is difficult as receipt via electronic methods do not require patrons to visit the circulation desk. Perhaps an e-mail with an invoice is sent before the item is received. Or the library has a system for online payment and an invoice is sent with a link to the site. No matter what method is used, it is best practice to "collect money for charges, if these are passed on to the patron, before handing out the material" (Boucher, 1997: 47). If the library has another billing and payment system in place, there is no reason to reinvent the wheel; the established practice should also be used by the interlibrary loan department.

Fees for extra services such as rush delivery should be charged to the patron. These fees should be significant enough to discourage multiple rush and special requests. Any overdue, damaged, and lost materials fees imposed by supplying institutions should also be passed along in full to patrons. Patrons should be charged for overdue materials whether or not the supplying library charges a fee. If the lending library does not charge, the fee should be the same as overdue fees for the libraries' own materials. This is also true for damaged and lost materials. Institutions should determine whether there is a maximum charge for these fees.

Policy Statements

- Reading Public Library charges $5.00 for each requested item. Fees are collected when the material is picked up at the circulation desk.
- Reading College does not charge for interlibrary loan.
- Reading College absorbs up to $20.00 of borrowing fees. If the lending library charges more than this amount, library staff will contact the patron.
- Patrons are responsible for all overdue, damaged, or lost item fees.

Management Strategies to Save Time and Resources

It is more difficult for small departments to save time on the borrowing side of interlibrary loan. Patrons will ask for what they want whether adequate staff is available to handle the requests or not. However, staff members can use time and money-saving measures to streamline borrowing operations. These include techniques such as using electronic requests as much as possible, automating verification by using electronic database requests, and most important, creating lists and profiles that will help borrowing processes run more smoothly.

Preparatory Work

After developing procedures for interlibrary borrowing, staff members should complete several preliminary tasks that will improve borrowing processes. These include creating cooperating library network charts, profiles and patron forms in WCRS, and forms for patrons on the library's Web site.

A chart of all of the networks to which the library belongs should be created first. As described previously, the chart should have each network OCLC symbol as well as a short description of the special services the network provides. The chart should be saved in an electronic departmental folder and printed out in for easy access while processing requests. Whenever network agreements are modified, the chart should be updated.

Developing borrowing regulations and procedures as well as a chart of cooperating networks will make it easier to create complete and accurate Constant Data profiles in WCRS. Using these profiles effectively will help make work in the system more efficient.

Constant Data profiles are also used to route requests when using WCRS patron-initiated service Direct Request. These requests do not necessarily have to be immediately routed to supplying libraries; they can also be sent to a review file. The two options for routing requests directly to supplying libraries in WCRS are "Direct-to-Lender," which sends requests using a borrowing library-supplied lending institution string, and "Direct-to-Profile," which uses Constant Data profiles to send requests to lenders or to the review file (OCLC, 2008). Systems that use OCLC's FirstSearch database aggregator automatically use the "Direct-to-Profile" option. Requests created outside of FirstSearch cannot use the Direct Request service unless they have certain hardware and software that can communicate with the OCLC system. Setting up this service is rather complicated and small departments should not try to do this unless they have adequate information technology resources to do so.

Receiving Patron Requests

Small interlibrary loan departments should be able to accept borrowing requests via e-mail, telephone, mail, and fax but the preferred method should be through an online form. This form can be supplied through WCRS or it can be a locally made HTML form that resides on the library Web site. No matter what type of form is used, small interlibrary loan departments should encourage patrons to use electronic rather than paper forms. Using publicly available electronic forms places the burden of keying in information on the patron rather than on interlibrary loan staff (Hilyer, 2002: 58), thus reference desk staff should always point patrons toward the electronic form.

Setting up the WCRS form should be part of the preparation tasks described previously. Locally made forms should include fields for complete bibliographic and patron information. Collecting complete information is easier electronically because HTML coding can be used to require users to fill out certain fields. To ensure that patrons fill out the correct information, it is recommended that small departments create two forms: one for book loans and another for photocopy requests. More information on developing these forms can be found in Chapter 9.

User Confidentiality

The national ILL code notes that it is the requesting libraries' responsibility to make sure that the user's identity remains confidential (American Library Association, 2008). If possible, borrowing libraries should use patron identification numbers when submitting requests to potential supplying libraries. It is not, however, an infringement of the code to use patrons' names on requests. If it is difficult for small departments to use ID numbers, then patrons' names should be used.

Because they are library records, interlibrary loan requests are confidential. When communicating with supplying libraries, it is not necessary to offer the identity of the requesting patron. The explanatory guidelines of the national code encourage institutions to create policies for preserving interlibrary loan records. If possible, patron information should be eliminated from any completed transaction records. Users' names on paper records should be re-dacted using dark permanent marker.

Verifying Requests

Verifying a request is less of a problem when patrons use biblio-graphic utilities and databases, such as the ones found in OCLC's FirstSearch, which automatically fill out request forms with the click of a mouse. When patrons key information into forms, how-ever, citation errors will inevitably occur.

Locally made ILL forms should require patrons to fill out as much information as needed for complete citations. Boucher's handbook lists the elements of correct citations for many different materials including books, articles, newspapers, dissertations and theses, and government documents. For example, citations for pe-riodical articles should include the title, volume, issue number or date, and year of the periodical as well as the author, title, and pages of the article (Boucher 1997: 16). Forms should require all of the pages of the article in case they are not in sequence.

Using this method of requiring certain fields in an HTML form to be completed means that most incomplete citations will result from patrons using indecipherable abbreviations in titles and transposition of numbers. Staff members can employ several tech-niques to investigate difficult citations. First, staff should contact the patron to find out more information about the request. Second, if they have the time, staff members can re-create patrons' searches using the library's databases. Hilyer writes that "many times the likely database the patron used can be determined simply by re-viewing the subject matter of the request" (Hilyer, 2002: 63).

Another technique is to use Google Scholar to conduct a key-word search for a periodical article. WorldCat.org and Google Books can be used for book searches. Finally, when searching for scholarly articles, try to find the author's CV on the Internet. This usually requires only a few keywords from the unverified request and a bit of ingenuity. Many scholars post their CVs online and these often have complete, searchable citation information. Although large departments might have the manpower to spend quite a bit of time verifying requests, small departments do not. If time is critical, contact the patron and let him or her know that the request cannot be filled until more complete citation information is received.

Managing Copyright

Chapter 3 included an extensive discussion of copyright law. The borrowing library must ensure that the library adheres to fair use guidelines. For small interlibrary loan departments, maintaining records to follow CONTU Guidelines is somewhat complicated. WCRS has no copyright tracking system, and therefore small departments must use a homegrown system. Chapter 9 includes an extensive discussion of how to use a spreadsheet to keep track of copyright.

Although this method is data entry heavy, it allows small departments to fulfill their responsibilities with regard to the CONTU Guidelines. Staff members will be able to tell at a glance if they are reaching the Rule of Five limit or are in danger of violating copyright law in some other manner. If this limit is reached, staff members should use the Copyright Clearance Center's Pay-Per-Use service. Note that this service does not require registration with the Center. If the library process is in danger of reaching the Rule of Five limit frequently, administrators should consider registering for the Center's Annual Licensing Service. Information regarding both of these services is available on the Copyright Clearance Center's Web site at copyright.com. Items on the copyright tracking spreadsheet should be deleted once the five-year mark is reached. Electronically received request files should be kept for three calendar years.

Overdue Materials

Patrons should be charged for overdue materials at the library's regular rate. This fee, along with any other fees that are assessed by the supplying library, should be added to the patron's ILS record. If the department does not normally use dummy records for returnable materials, they may want to add them for overdue and recalled materials. This would allow the ILS to calculate any charges. Otherwise, these fees can be tracked manually and then added to the patron's record as a miscellaneous charge.

Damaged Materials

If items are damaged when they are returned, patrons should be charged the library's lost material replacement fee and also informed that they will have to pay any additional charges that are assessed by the supplying library. Train circulation desk staff to inspect ILL returns for damage when returned. If patrons are not present when the item is received by staff, they should be sent an e-mail informing them that they have been charged for damage to the material. This fee should also be added to the patron's ILS record.

Other Borrowing Policy Considerations

As with lending services, co-operating network libraries can help small interlibrary loan departments save money on borrowing services. Small institutions should try to join as many reciprocal borrowing networks as possible. It is especially advantageous if the libraries in these networks are located nearby.

Borrowing policies should also include average turnaround times for requests. One method to use to find the average turnaround time is to conduct a survey over a month noting the date requests are sent and subsequently received. The average of these time spans should be listed in the borrowing policy.

Finally, interlibrary loan staff in small departments should be aware of commercial document delivery services. Suppliers such as Infotrieve (www.infotrieve.com) and Dissertation Express (disexpress.umi.com/dxweb) will provide a wide range of documents for a substantial fee. Some document delivery services, including InfoQuest (www.lib.auburn.edu/infoquest) and Michigan Information Transfer Source (MITS) (www.lib.umich.edu/mits), are run by large universities to provide services to the public and give their respective libraries an additional revenue stream. In small departments, these services should only be used as a last resort and all fees should generally be passed on to the patron. A comprehensive list of document delivery suppliers is available on the ShareILL Web site (www.illweb.org) under "Document Suppliers."

Streamlining Borrowing Procedures

Small interlibrary loan departments should develop borrowing and lending procedures with an eye toward discarding inefficient practices. Almost all aspects of the borrowing transaction should be conducted electronically. Much of the burden for entering data and verifying citations should be placed on the patron and not on departmental staff.

Completing adequate preparatory work, such as filling out profiles in WCRS and creating charts of cooperating library services, will help staff members save time in the long run. Small interlibrary loan departments often lack the technological capabilities, such as full-featured ILS and full-scale electronic document delivery systems found at larger institutions. Recent technological developments, such as the availability of WorldCat.org, allow small ILL departments to more easily provide patrons with needed materials.

References

American Library Association. 2008. *Interlibrary Loan Code for the United States*. Available: www.ala.org/ala/mgrps/divs/rusa/resources/guidelines/interlibrary.cfm (accessed July 30, 2009).

Boucher, Virginia. 1997. *Interlibrary Loan Practices Handbook*. Chicago: American Library Association.

Brumley, Rebecca. 2006. *The Reference Librarian's Policies, Forms, Guidelines, and Procedures Handbook with CD-ROM*. New York: Neal-Schuman.

Hilyer, Lee Andrew. 2002. *Interlibrary Loan and Document Delivery in the Larger Academic Library*. Binghamton, NY: The Haworth Press.

OCLC. 2008. *WorldCat Resource Sharing Documentation*. Available: www.oclc.org/us/en/support/documentation/resourcesharing/ (accessed July 30, 2009).

ILL and Document Delivery Technology Systems

Technology and the Small Interlibrary Loan Department

Access to state-of-the-art technology is a major dividing line between large and small interlibrary loan departments. Software companies invest thousands of dollars into creating and improving ILL delivery and management systems for high volume operations. Unfortunately, these systems come with a price tag that puts them out of reach for small departments. It is difficult to justify spending thousands or even hundreds of dollars each year to manage only a few hundred transactions.

This does not mean that small departments do not use any technology but their choice of which systems to use is more limited. Small ILL departments often cobble together systems using various software packages instead of buying an integrated interlibrary loan management system. These systems have several disadvantages: they often do not track copyright clearances and lack functionality and customizability. Hybrid systems do not work as smoothly as commercially developed ones, but they do improve efficiency within the department.

Although many small interlibrary departments may not be able to afford ILL technology solutions, it is important for all staff members who provide ILL services to be familiar with commercially available systems. Discussions and reviews of ILL technology appear throughout general library literature and tracking information from these systems (i.e., the Ariel IP address) sometimes appears on borrowing requests. If a library's circumstances change (either financially or in terms of transaction volume) it is good to know which tools are available to streamline workflows.

This chapter is divided into four sections. The first gives a general introduction to some of the current technological issues in interlibrary loan. The second section provides a brief overview of several ILL standards including the ISO ILL Protocol and Z39.50. The third section discusses how to choose technology for the small interlibrary loan department. The final section is divided into four parts. The first discusses two bibliographic utilities, WorldCat Resource Sharing and DOCLINE. The second looks at standalone Interlibrary Loan Management Systems (IMS). The third part discusses document delivery software. The final section gives a brief overview of ILL modules that can be purchased in conjunction with integrated library systems (ILS).

Note that small interlibrary loan departments do not need any of these software systems to run efficiently and provide good customer service. The following chapter discusses inexpensive technology solutions that can be used to run a paperless interlibrary loan office. The terms "software," "technology," and "solutions" are used loosely and interchangeably throughout the chapter.

Technology and Interlibrary Loan

As with everything in the library world, interlibrary loan is intimately connected with information technology. Chapter 1 mentioned some of the innovations in technology that made ILL more efficient, including the teletypewriter, the fax machine, and e-mail. Other technologies that revolutionized the world of interlibrary loan include scanners, printers, and networked personal computers. Although some of these tools, such as the teletypewriter, are no longer used, others have become ubiquitous and it is difficult to think of running an interlibrary loan department without them.

Library software companies have also produced many products for the interlibrary loan market. These include document transmission software such as Atlas Systems's Odyssey and modules that work with integrated library systems such as Ex Libris's Voyager. One of the most important types of software for interlibrary loan is the interlibrary loan management systems (IMS). Described in detail in section two of this chapter, IMS, like ILLiad and Clio, not only track transactions, they also create reports, monitor copyright information, produce use statistics, and provide user-friendly processing interfaces for both departmental staff and patrons.

Unfortunately, many of these systems are quite expensive and require specialized expertise to manage. As mentioned in Chapter 2, "Special Topics for Small Interlibrary Loan and Document Delivery Departments," both money and technological expertise are often lacking in the small institutions that house small ILL departments. This does not mean that small departments should not consider the solutions discussed in this chapter; it simply means that they must choose wisely.

In 2000, Mary Jackson published the only comprehensive handbook that describes interlibrary loan technology. The changes since then are staggering: seven of the products no longer exist, entire companies (such as Endeavor) were bought by competitors, and many more products use the ISO ILL Protocol. Jackson notes five products that are specifically aimed at the small department. Of the five mentioned, two (TLC Total Library Computerization and Winnebago Spectrum Union Catalog) no longer exist. Web Collection Plus has been superseded by Follett's Destiny Library Manager. The two remaining products, KLAS and Mandarin3, are briefly noted in the ILS ILL modules part of the fourth section of this chapter.

Interlibrary Loan Standards

Technology standards allow communication between electronic networks. Several international and national standards directly affect interlibrary loan. This is not surprising as providing interlibrary loan is impossible without communication between institutions. Three standards are of particular importance: the International Standards Organization Interlibrary Loan Protocol, the National Information Standards Organization Circulation Interchange Protocol, and the Z39.50 Protocol. A brief, nontechnical overview of these three standards follows. This section also provides a brief introduction to link resolvers, a technology that has revolutionized access to electronic materials.

International Standards Organization Interlibrary Loan Protocol (ISO ILL Protocol)

In her introduction to her handbook on interlibrary loan technology, Mary Jackson (2000) discusses the importance of the ISO ILL Protocol. Briefly mentioned in Chapter 1, it will be explained in a bit more detail here, as it is important to know what it means when a product is "ILL Protocol Compliant." "Protocol" in this context refers to the peer-to-peer language syntax libraries use to communicate with each other. The ILL protocol (ISO 10160/ 10161) is maintained by the ILL Application Standards Maintenance Agency and can be read in its entirety at www.lac-bac .gc.ca/iso/ill/standard.htm.

The protocol includes many technical elements that are probably interesting only to people who develop computer systems. However, other parts of the protocol are encountered by almost any staff person who conducts ILL. For example, the "Reasons for

No," which indicate why a supplying library cannot send a requested item, were originally created by the ILL Protocol Implementers Group and are continually updated and sanctioned by the International Standards Organization. When a product is ISO ILL compliant, it means that it adheres to all of the technical definitions required by the standard. Some products, such as ILLiad, are protocol compliant, whereas others (like DOCLINE) are not. It is not necessary for all ILL software to be protocol compliant to connect to each other; the protocol simply eases communication between machines at different libraries.

National Information Standards Organization (NISO) Circulation Interchange Protocol (NCIP)

The NCIP allows institutions to exchange information for circulating items. According to Jackson, it includes three application areas: "direct consortial borrowing, self-service circulation, and interaction between circulation and ILL systems" (Jackson, 2000: 9). It essentially automates communication between circulation systems and interlibrary loan systems. NCIP uses XML for message exchange.

Jackson's introduction, which was written before NCIP's implementation, provides a concise explanation of how the protocol works:

> . . . NCIP will permit ILL lending staff to check out a book on their circulation system and have that circulation system update their ILL Protocol-compliant ILL system. The ISO ILL message that the item has been shipped is sent to the borrower's Protocol-compliant system, which may create a temporary record in the borrower's circulation system to permit patrons to check out the borrowed ILL book on their local circulation system. (Jackson, 2000: 9)

Z39.50

The Z39.50 protocol is familiar to anyone who has ever set up an OPAC. Z39.50 "allows programs at one site to conduct searches of remote catalogs in support of interlibrary loan processes and to retrieve search results that are in a form suitable for subsequent postprocessing by these same programs" (Lynch, 1995: 146). This protocol allows users to search several catalogs through one interface.

Link Resolvers

Link resolvers are a type of software that points users to electronically available materials. "Link resolver software brings together information about the cited resource, the user, and the library's many subscriptions, policies and services" (McDonald and Van de Velde, 2004). When a user searches for a particular article and clicks on the link resolver button, the software uses the OpenURL Framework to find out if the article is available to the user and then either creates a link to the article or to the library OPAC. OpenURL, another NISO standard, is used to send metadata regarding information resources.

 Link resolvers are often very expensive but libraries should consider purchasing them if possible. Using a link resolver can cut down on the amount staff time spent reviewing requests for materials that the library already owns. Link resolvers can also be used to pre-populate ILL request forms which can greatly reduce citation errors.

Criteria for Selecting Cost-effective Technology

In his book on library technology, the *Library Technology Companion*, John Burke (2009: 42–43) lists nine criteria for evaluating new technology purchases in libraries. It is important to consider all nine criteria when choosing technology for any interlibrary loan departments. This section addresses the nine principles in light of the issues that are unique to small interlibrary loan departments.

- "Is the technology suitable?"

  Technology has greatly improved efficiency in interlibrary loan departments. The question for small departments is whether the solutions are suitable for a small number of transactions. Also, department staff must ask whether the technological benefits outweigh the costs. For example, although it might be easier to push documents to patrons using Ariel, if you only send out 100 documents per year, does the cost of the software outweigh the staff time that it takes to send e-mails?

- "Is the technology close to obsolescence?"

  This is vitally important for small interlibrary loan departments that have few resources to waste on obsolete technology. Perhaps technologies that are on their way out can be combined with newer ones. For example, when a fax machine stops working, does it make sense to buy a new one when fewer ILL departments use faxes for sending and receiving documents? Might it make more sense to buy a scanner/printer/copier/fax? Technology changes very quickly and it is important to keep this in mind when buying equipment.

- "How durable is the technology?"

  Buying new scanners and printers every year does not make much sense for small departments. Be sure to buy equipment that stands up to regular use. As Burke notes, "Technology is expensive enough that it should be around long enough to justify its expense" (Burke, 2009: 42).

- "Does the technology fit into the library's environment?"

  Burke asks this question both literally and figuratively. "Is the item something that fits the mission of the library? Can a piece of equipment fit into the space of the library?" (Burke, 2009: 42) Because many small interlibrary loan offices do not occupy separate physical space, perhaps the equipment can be shared with other library staff members. ILL, as with all aspects of library work, is patron centered. If buying the equipment or software does not advance the interlibrary loan department mission to patrons, it might not be necessary. For small interlibrary loan departments, it is probably more important to have a scanner that performs well rather than a state-of-the-art scanner with numerous bells and whistles.

• "What implications does the technology have for training?"

In small institutions it can be difficult for staff members to receive adequate training for new products. Many software developers offer training with their products but these are often quite expensive. If it is too difficult to learn how to use the product then it is probably not worth the expense.

• "What maintenance, upgrading, or updating needs does the technology have?"

When evaluating technology contracts, remember to look for any regular maintenance fees. These can significantly change overall expenditures for the products. Sometimes hardware must be upgraded at the same time as software and the costs for hardware upgrades are not always included in the interlibrary loan budget allocations. Finally, when purchasing software, ask about support. As companies upgrade products, older versions are usually no longer supported. This means that any problems must be solved through other means. Small departments should carefully consider whether their budgets allow continual upgrading. If they do not, support issues should be addressed before purchasing the product.

• "If the technology has problems, are people available locally (within the library or its community) who can provide support?"

As mentioned in Chapter 2, technology support is often a difficult problem for small institutions and finding competent support is often impossible. In a small interlibrary loan department, it is important that any software bought for the department can be supported by the institution's technology team.

Not thinking about technological support ahead of time can lead to cost overruns over time.

• "How does the price of the technology compare with similar technologies?"

It is not necessary to use any commercially developed interlibrary loan technology to provide high-quality service to patrons. The software described in the fourth section of this chapter can vary widely in price. It is important to consider all options before making any purchasing decisions. Hardware can also have wildly different price points. Burke's book includes an entire chapter on how to find out about library technologies. He discusses information sources that describe what is available to Web sites that give product reviews. Once again, it is important to think through any purchase before it is made. Burke writes that the technology's "ability to fit the need should outweigh discussions of price" (Burke, 2009: 43).

• "Is this technology the most appropriate way to provide this information or service?"

Unfortunately for small interlibrary loan departments when it comes to software the answer to this question is almost always yes. Commercially developed software is made for interlibrary loan and it will make staff members' lives easier. Cost is usually the factor that outweighs appropriateness. Hardware is a bit more complicated as a lot of it can be shared with other departments in the library. For example, if the interlibrary loan department cannot justify getting a new server perhaps it can also be used for electronic reserve. This might rationalize the cost of such an expensive piece of hardware.

To answer these questions, it is important to have a good analysis of the department. Examine statistics gathered to better determine which technologies might work for your individual circumstance. For example, if a department is sending out comparatively more documents, perhaps it makes sense to invest in a document delivery system. Burke's advice on this point deserves to be quoted at length:

We cannot evaluate whether or not a given technology is useful to our situation unless we know what need it is meant to address. Sadly, there are situations in which a new technology is chosen and implemented due to "technolust" (choosing technology due to its glitz rather than actual need) and then never used. Start with a need, and then base your evaluation on how well a given technology meets it. (Burke, 2009: 39)

Interlibrary Loan and Document Delivery Technology Solutions

As mentioned earlier, one of the problems that small interlibrary loan departments encounter is a lack of information technology support. With this in mind, each of the overviews below includes a summary of the hardware and/or software needed to use the product. Sometimes this information is not readily available as companies often consider information architecture to be a trade secret. Because technology changes so rapidly, readers are encouraged to visit the respective Web sites of the product manufacturers to discover more information on the systems and software.

It is sometimes difficult to obtain pricing information for these systems because companies want potential customers to fill out order forms or send in Requests for Proposals. In this situation, small interlibrary loan departments are encouraged to contact the product manufacturers directly. Once again, please note that none of these systems are necessary to run an efficient and customer service oriented ILL department.

Bibliographic Utilities

A bibliographic utility is an organization or network that provides a database of resources, member organizations, and holdings information in order to facilitate access, resource sharing, and cataloging. They often grew out of cooperative cataloging projects. Over time, vendors added various applications to the utilities including several that are used for interlibrary loan processing. These utilities are not true interlibrary loan management systems but do offer some functions. They can be used to find, request, and track ILL materials. Bibliographic utilities' technological specifications are minimal and generally only require a networked computer with high-speed broadband access.

OCLC WorldCat Resource Sharing

www.oclc.org/resourcesharing/default.htm

Overview

OCLC World Cat Resource Sharing is a lending network of more than 7,500 libraries. OCLC provides Web-based software that is fully integrated into its both WorldCat and OCLC's FirstSearch database aggregator. Patrons and staff members use the WorldCat union catalog or the database to find materials. Small interlibrary loan departments that have OCLC WorldCat Resource Sharing, but not an IMS, should maximize their use of the Resource Sharing software to make operations more efficient.

Pricing

Pricing information for WorldCat Resource Sharing is only available through OCLC's regional service providers.

Features

Since its introduction in 1979, OCLC has added many features to Resource Sharing. Some of the features listed on the Web site include constant data records that alleviate the need to type in the same lender/borrower information numerous times, instant access to the ILL policies of other libraries, and access to OCLC's interlibrary loan fee management (IFM) system. Other features include direct links to the Copyright Clearance Center, the ability to automatically deflect requests that your institution does not wish to fulfill, and as mentioned in Chapter 2, direct request, non-mediated, resource sharing. WorldCat Resource Sharing complies with the ISO ILL protocol.

Resource Sharing does not electronically deliver documents, it does not have a customizable Web interface for non-FirstSearch requests, and it does not keep statistics in real time. Most important, Resource Sharing does not track copyright clearances.

DOCLINE

www.nlm.nih.gov/docline/

Overview

DOCLINE is the bibliographic utility system created by the National Library of Medicine for medical libraries. The system seeks to "provide improved document delivery service among libraries in the National Network of Libraries of Medicine® (NN/LM®) by linking journal holdings to efficiently route the requests to potential lending libraries on behalf of the borrower." (National Library of Medicine, 2008). The National Library of Medicine also runs an interlibrary loan service although it is supposed to be "the library of last resort."

Pricing

DOCLINE is a free service to medical libraries. Eligibility requirements are posted on the Web site.

Features

DOCLINE's system has three modules: institutions, serial holdings, and requests. These modules enable DOCLINE member libraries to efficiently find, request, and borrow articles. As with OCLC it is incumbent upon member institutions to keep their institution and serial holdings records up to date. DOCLINE offers quarterly summary activity reports and more detailed annual reports. The Electronic Fund Transfer System (EFTS) is similar to OCLC's Interlibrary Management Fee system and reduces the need for invoicing and direct money transfer between institutions. DOCLINE member libraries may also join FreeShare, a reciprocal borrowing service. FreeShare libraries agree to provide all requests free of charge to other members. The National Library of Medicine also has a service called Loansome Doc that allows individuals to order documents through DOCLINE libraries even if they do not have access to DOCLINE's system.

Interlibrary Loan Management Systems (IMS)

Interlibrary loan management systems (IMS) are database-driven software systems that manage ILL electronically. Complete IMS differ from bibliographic utilities such as the OCLC Resource Sharing system because they can also manage copyright restrictions, deliver documents electronically, and create statistical reports. They can be an expensive investment for a small interlibrary loan department. Even with this caveat, small departments that can afford an IMS should consider purchasing one of these systems as they greatly increase efficiency.

Clio

www.cliosoftware.com

Overview

Clio Software is a family-owned company founded in 1996. The IMS was originally developed for University of California at Davis. At the moment Clio does not conform to ISO ILL Protocol but the Web site states that compliance will be added in the near future. There are two packages: Clio, which provides basic ILL productivity and management software for staff, and Clio Advanced, which adds a customizable interface for patrons.

Pricing

Clio is the most affordable of the IMS listed here. Its current prices start at $500 for the initial licensing fee and $350 for the annual maintenance fee.

Technology

Clio works on Windows machines and uses the Microsoft Access database system. ClioAdvance requires its own server and uses either ColdFusion or PHP.

Features

The basic Clio package includes two applications "Clio" and "ClioRequest." Clio is the management application that handles ILL requests, creates and manages invoices and payments, and pushes notifications to patrons. It handles administrative tasks such as creating reports and statistics. ClioRequest is a Web-based request interface for patron requests. ClioAdvanced also has several applications and is an extension of ClioRequest. ClioWeb enhances the functionality the patron interface by adding the ability to check the status of requests and to renew materials as well as the capability to pick up electronically delivered documents. This latter function is part of the staff-side ClioEDelivery application that integrates Clio with Ariel.

Clio works with both OCLC Resource Sharing and DOCLINE and also supports unmediated patron requests.

OCLC ILLiad

www.oclc.org/us/en/illiad/default.htm

Overview

OCLC ILLiad was originally created by Atlas Systems for Virginia Tech and bought by OCLC in 2000. OCLC now holds exclusive distribution rights to ILLiad. The system was specifically created for high-volume institutions and is priced accordingly. Atlas Systems also created the Odyssey electronic transmission software discussed later.

Pricing

According to an article published in the *Journal of the Medial Library Association*, OCLC ILLiad costs $2,317–$5,793 annually (You, Lynch, and McCollum, 2008: 177).

Technology

Staff-side software runs on Windows machines. ILLiad requires three separate products to operate: Microsoft SQL server, Windows Server, and Internet Information Service. OCLC and Atlas Systems recommend using a separate server for these applications. Institutions can also use Atlas Systems (Software as Service) hosted servers.

Features

ILLiad is fully integrated with both OCLC Resource Sharing and the Odyssey document delivery system and offers some functionality with DOCLINE. Features include real-time statistics, electronic document delivery to patrons' desktops, and a flexible Web interface for both staff and patrons. Patrons can create profiles to track requests and pick up documents. ILLiad also includes reports that can be downloaded directly to Microsoft Excel and a Web circulation module for monitoring returnable materials. It supports both mediated and unmediated requests.

Relais International ILL

www.relais-intl.com/relais/home/ill.htm

Overview

Relais International, a Canadian company, offers two IMS products. One, Relais Enterprise, is comprehensive and includes scanning and document delivery components. The other, Relais ILL is specifically targeted to small operations and offers fewer customization options. It should be noted that Relais defines small as less than 50,000 transactions annually. This brief overview focuses on Relais ILL.

Pricing

Relais International's Web site does not offer pricing information.

Technology

Relais ILL requires Microsoft SQL Server Desktop Engine (MSDE) database. A license for MSDE is included with the product. It can also run on MS SQL and Oracle but licenses for these applications must be purchased separately. Relais ILL also requires a Web server. The Web site's technical overview notes that some knowledge of Crystal Reports is helpful for customizing reports. Relais also offers a hosted server (Software as a Service) option.

Features

According to the Web site product description, Relais ILL is a pre-packaged solution for smaller ILL departments. It offers all of the functionality of any IMS including patron request forms, request tracking, accounting functions and statistical management. The Web site's comparison chart notes that Relais ILL

> comes pre-packaged and requires much less administrative knowledge in terms of the Database, Server, etc., whereas Enterprise requires special training and specialized support personnel. It should be ready to use, out of the box. Essentially, Relais has gone through & effectively chosen the most common settings for small libraries so that these libraries do not need to worry about all the administrative details. (Relais International, 2009)

Relais ILL is ISO ILL protocol-compliant and is in the process of supporting NCIP. It is fully integrated with OCLC and can receive (but not send) requests to DOCLINE.

QuickDOC

nnlm.gov/quickdoc/

Overview

QuickDOC is IMS that works exclusively with DOCLINE. It is maintained by the developer, Jay Daly of Beth Israel Deaconess Medical Center of Harvard Medical School.

Pricing

Quick DOC costs $299.95 for new users, $149.95 for users with fewer than 6,000 transactions per year, and has an $89.95 annual fee.

Technology

The program uses Microsoft Data Access Components.

Features

QuickDOC has two components: QD Portal and QuickDOC Program. "The QD Portal program saves DOCLINE transactions (borrow, lend, and Loansome Doc) automatically for importing into the QuickDOC program. The QuickDOC program includes a database for maintaining records, searching, editing, preparing electronic funds transfer systems (EFTS) files, statistics reports, and billing functions" (Munson and Hill, 2003: 377). According to QuickDOC's Web site, Daly hopes to merge QDPortal into QuickDOC in the near future.

Document Delivery Systems

Document delivery systems are not comprehensive interlibrary loan systems. Instead, they automate the process of sending documents electronically. They essentially replace fax machines by offering faster service, higher quality documents, and the convenience of desktop delivery. Remember that these systems do not communicate with each other. For example, if an institution does not have an ILS, it must use Ariel software to send documents to Ariel sites. Odyssey software does not interact with Ariel Software.

Ariel

http://corporate.infotrieve.com/ariel

Overview

Ariel, originally created in the 1980s by the Research Libraries Group, has been owned and distributed by Infotrieve, Inc. since 2003. Infotrieve specializes in content management technology. Ariel uses existing network connections to transmit PDFs over the Internet using MIME and FTP.

Pricing

Infotrieve offers two pricing models (perpetual licenses and annual subscription) and two types of applications (full and receive only.) Perpetual full version licenses are $1,295 whereas receive-only licenses are $795. Annual subscriptions for the full version are $498 per year and receive-only subscriptions are $298 per year.

Technology

Ariel requires a printer, a scanner, access to high-speed broadband Internet, and plenty of hard drive space.

Features

Ariel can scan, view, send, receive, and print documents while maintaining all bibliographic and transaction information. Interlibrary loan staff members are usually familiar with the Ariel network addresses (XXX.XXX.XXX.XXX where the Xs are numbers) that are often listed in the "Shipping Address" portion of a borrowing libraries request. These addresses are used to direct documents to the correct library. After receiving an item, staff members can then transmit documents to a patron's desktop using

MIME e-mail or post them on the Web. Institutions can only ship to an Ariel address if they use Ariel or Prospero software or if they have an IMS that supports shipping to Ariel IP addresses.

Odyssey

www.atlas-sys.com/products/odyssey/

Overview and Pricing

Odyssey, produced by Atlas systems, has been available free of charge since 2005. It uses the Open Odyssey protocol to transmit documents to other Odyssey and OCLC Iliad sites.

Technology

Odyssey requires a scanner, a printer, broadband Internet access, and plenty of hard drive space.

Features

Odyssey is fully integrated with OCLC ILLiad. It includes scanning software and facilitates the process of sending and receiving electronic documents. Odyssey does not post documents on the Web for electronic delivery to patrons. It also does not include a patron notification application.

Prospero

bones.med.ohio-state.edu/prospero/

Overview and Pricing

Prospero is a free, open-source document delivery system created by the Prior Health Sciences Library of the Ohio State University. It was originally created to work with Ariel but now functions as a stand-alone system. It transmits documents to and from Ariel and Prospero sites via FTP. As with all open-source software, the creators do not provide technical support and it is unclear if it will be updated in the future.

Technology

As it is open source software, anyone can download the necessary files to run Prospero. It requires a scanner for the staff module and a Web server with Perl on the server side. A review article notes that "most libraries will need to rely on institution information technology . . . or systems staff to install and configure Prospero" (Morgen and Hersey, 2008: 381).

Features

Prospero captures and queues electronic documents to receive and deliver to patrons. It automatically alerts patrons when a document is available. It includes patron authentication and limits the number of times an article can be viewed. According to several review articles, it is very easy to use. It is clear that Infotrieve increased the functionality of Ariel due to direct competition from Prospero.

Integrated Library Systems (ILS) Modules

Interlibrary loan modules are optional add-ons for their respective ILS. They are not available as separate products and are usually only purchased by large ILL departments. The top five most popular ILS (Ex Libris Aleph, Sirsi Dynix Unicorn and Horizon, Innovative Interfaces Millennium, and Ex Libris Voyager) as well as one ILS often purchased by small libraries (Auto-Graphics Agent Verso) all have ILL modules. Jackson's handbook reviews two other modules that are available for small libraries, KLAS and Mandarin3. One of the most popular Open Source ILS, Koha from LibLime, does not include an interlibrary loan module.

These modules are similar to IMS and help manage interlibrary loan transactions. An extension of the circulation module, they track borrowed materials, add fines and fees to transactions, and can keep statistical reports. The modules make it easy for patrons to keep track of borrowed materials using their accounts in the library's ILS.

Using Technology

It is important to remember that technology is only a tool. It can improve efficiency but it is almost never absolutely necessary. If it is possible for managers of small departments to purchase the products mentioned in this chapter then they should seriously consider doing so. The next chapter offers suggestions for running a paperless interlibrary loan office using readily available (and often inexpensive) technology.

References and Works Consulted

Boyd, Morag, Sandy Roe, and Sarah E. George. 2006. "Beyond Article Linking: Using OpenURL in Creative Ways." *The Serials Librarian* 50, no. 3/4: 221–226.

Breeding, Marshall. "Automation System Marketplace 2008. Opportunity Out of Turmoil." *Library Journal* (April 1, 2008). Available: www.libraryjournal.com (accessed November 2, 2008).

Burk, Roberta. 2006. "Self-Service Interlibrary Loan: A Primer for Reference Staff." *The Reference Librarian*, no. 93: 78–82.

Burke, John J. 2009. *Neal-Schuman Library Technology Companion: A Basic Guide for Library Staff*, 3rd Edition. New York: Neal-Schuman.

Clark, Heather. 2007. "ILL Management Software: Fare to Fuel Your Productivity." *Action for Libraries* 33, no. 1. Available: www.bcr.org (accessed October 17, 2008).

Hilyer, Lee Andrew. 2006. *Interlibrary Loan and Document Delivery: Best Practices for Operating and Managing Interlibrary Loan Services in All Libraries*. Binghamton, NY: The Haworth Press.

Jackson, Mary E. 2000. *Interlibrary Loan and Resource Sharing Products: An Overview of Current Features and Functionality*. Chicago: American Library Association.

Lynch, C. A. 1995. "System Architecture and Networking Issues in Implementing the North American Interlibrary Loan and Document Delivery (NAILDD) Initiative." In *The Future of Resource Sharing* (pp. 145–167), edited by Shirley K. Baker and Mary E. Jackson. Binghamton, NY: The Haworth Press.

McDonald, John, and Eric F. Van de Velde. 2004. "The Lure of Linking: Link Resolvers Are Essential to Getting Optimal Usage of Electronic Content and Linking 101." *Library Journal* (January 1). Available: www.libraryjournal.com (accessed November 4, 2008).

Morgen, Evelyn, and Denise Hersey. 2003 "Prospero 2.0." *Journal of the Medical Library Association*, 91, no. 3 (July): 381.

Munson, Kurt I., and Thomas W. Hill. 2003. "QuickDOC for Windows 2.1.1." *Journal of the Medical Library Association* 91, no. 3 (July): 377.

National Library of Medicine. 2008. "Fact Sheet: DOCLINE." Available: www.nlm.nih.gov/pubs/factsheets/docline.html (accessed July 30, 2009).

Nevins, Kate. 1998. "An Ongoing Revolution: Resource Sharing and OCLC." *Journal of Library Administration* 25, no. 2/3: 65–71.

Norton, Melanie, and Michelle Stover. 2003. "OCLC ILLiad." *Journal of the Medical Library Association* 91, no. 3 (July): 379.

Relais International. 2009. "Relais Product Comparison." Available: www.relais-intl.com/relais/home/productscomparison.htm (accessed July 30, 2009).

Schnell, Eric. 2002. "Prospero." *Open Source Software for Librarians: An Open Source for Libraries Collaboration* (pp. 19–29). LITA Guide #9. Chicago: LITA.

Whitlock, Margaret, and Alice Edwards. 2003. "Clio 3.5." *Journal of the Medical Library Association* 91, no. 3 (July): 378.

You, Tau, Frances Lynch, and Dan McCollum. 2008. "OCLC ILLiad." *Journal of the Medical Library Association* 96, no. 2 (April): 177.

Going Paperless for Cheap

In the not-so-distant past, all libraries conducted interlibrary loan on paper. Reading through older interlibrary loan manuals quickly leads to mental images of ILL offices overstuffed with piles of paper. Although ILL processes can still consume a large amount of paper, ILL is no longer a paper-driven service. Computer technology, particularly the systems discussed in Chapter 8, has completely transformed the ILL department office. In many libraries, the only nonelectronic part of ILL is the physical transfer of books from one library to another. All other aspects of ILL, from requesting items to document delivery, are handled electronically.

This chapter discusses how small interlibrary loan departments can create a paperless interlibrary loan department without using any of the commercially developed systems described in the previous chapter. It offers suggestions for easy to find and operate hardware and software as well as processing procedures. The chapter describes an idealized situation in which all of the software used is available for free. In reality, most small departments would probably develop a hybrid system that combines commercially developed applications such as WorldCat Resource Sharing or DOCLINE with free software. Even though using these home-grown systems is not as elegant as the commercially developed software packages, they allow small departments to accomplish the same tasks as large ones without spending a lot of money or printing out a lot of paper.

The Paperless Office

For more than 30 years, the business world has promised that the paperless office is on the horizon. Although most work situations are still not paperless, ILL service is an ideal area in which to implement the paperless office within the library. ILL, both borrowing and lending, requires five transactions: receiving a request, finding the material requested, transferring the material, tracking, and accounting. None of these transactions requires either paper or the systems listed in Chapter 8.

With a bit of ingenuity, basic knowledge of ubiquitous office software, and, if staff is feeling particular ambitious, some familiarity with HTML forms, anyone can create a paperless ILL system. These techniques and procedures can also be used with the systems described in Chapter 8. Staff members should pick and choose from the following suggestions as needed. For example, if the department uses OCLC WorldCat Resource Sharing to handle most requests, personal information software can be set to alert a staff member to check the lending queue on a regular basis. For many situations, office productivity software can mimic the functions of commercially developed interlibrary loan management systems.

To achieve a paperless office, small interlibrary loan department staff should be encouraged to think before printing. Many people tend to print documents out of habit or because they believe that it will be easier to accomplish tasks with a piece of paper. Stacks of paper are a visual and physical reminder of both work that has been completed and tasks that still need to be done. It is tempting to print lending and borrowing requests in order to process them. However, except for physically retrieving materials from the shelf, almost all of the request searches can be accomplished online. Applying the "think before you print" principle will help save paper in any office situation.

ILL and Document Delivery Technologies for Tight Budgets

Most libraries provide office productivity software such as Microsoft Office to their staff members. These products are the foundation for creating a paperless office on a tight budget. Even if the software is not provided by the institution, open source productivity software, such as OpenOffice, Zoho, or Google Docs, is available for free on the Internet. The low budget paperless ILL department requires four types of software and three pieces of hardware.

Software

Personal information software, such as MS Outlook, is generally used to track appointments, monitor daily tasks, and manage e-mail. The personal information software e-mail client should be used to receive requests whereas the task reminder function serves as a prod to review requests in a timely manner. If MS Outlook is not available, free calendar systems such as Google Calendar or Windows Live can be used. These programs, which include task reminder functions, are fairly intuitive and can be used by a computer novice.

Word-processing software can be used to create bookstraps, labels, and templates for notices. Many offices use MS Word or Corel WordPerfect; however, if these are not available, it is recommended that departments use an open source program such as OpenOffice Writer.Freely available Web-based applications such as Google Docs or Zoho do have some templates for labels, but they do not have the same flexibility as full-function word-processing software.

Spreadsheet software such as MS Excel or OpenOffice Calc is the third type of software needed to create a paperless office.

Spreadsheets are generally used to crunch numbers and data, but they can also be used to track transactions using any assigned criteria. Because database technology has a higher learning curve, the author encourages the use of spreadsheets (a type of flat database) instead of database software such as MS Access for keeping track of ILL. The tracking method described below assumes a beginner's level familiarity with spreadsheet software. However, if staff members are familiar with database software, they are encouraged to use it as it provides superior functionality.

Finally, the paperless ILL department needs scanning software. The optical character recognition (OCR) software that comes with most scanners has greatly improved over the past few years; therefore, it is not necessary to buy any special software. The bundled scanning software should also be able to scan materials into PDF format for electronic document delivery. If it is not, open source and other freely available PDF creation software is also available on the Web. Staff members should be very familiar with the particular software used in the ILL office. This knowledge will help save time when filling requests.

Hardware

A basic workstation with Internet access is the first piece of hardware needed for the paperless office. The software products mentioned above do not require large amounts of memory or fast processing speeds. Any recent computer model should have adequate computing power. Note that PDFs are often large files and require large amounts of hard drive space. It is recommended that the workstation PC be connected to a shared network drive or, alternatively, that the ILL workstation has a dedicated external hard drive that can be used to save scanned documents.

The second piece of equipment that ILL departments need is a scanner. In order to save money and to have a machine that can be used for many different tasks, small departments should consider buying an all-in-one color inkjet printer/scanner/copier/fax. This machine can be used by the entire library staff. Prices for all-in-ones have dropped dramatically over the past few years and it should not be difficult to find a reasonably priced model that comes with adequate software.

Finally, the workstation should have a printer in order to print out labels and supplies. This printer should be a laser printer rather than inkjet. Laser printers have a higher initial cost but are less costly on a per-sheet basis. As a way to save money, some departments might be tempted to buy only the all-in-one printer/scanner/copier/fax instead of buying a separate laser printer. However, printing labels and bookstraps on the inkjet will cost more over time. It makes more sense, and will probably lower costs over the long run, if the department buys both types of printers. The all-in-one can be used for scanning and any color print jobs, whereas the laser printer can be used for everyday printing.

Note that these technologies will not allow a small interlibrary loan and document delivery departments to meet ILL Code for the United States as discussed in Chapter 3. They will, however, allow the department to provide services at the lowest cost possible.

Creating Online Forms for the Library Web Site

With these tools, any staff member can begin to implement the paperless office. Setting up the templates and forms should not take more than one day. Templates for bookstraps, labels, and notices should be created in the word-processing software and saved in a common folder for later use (see Figures 9-1, 9-2, and 9-3 for examples).

Creating online forms and making them "live" on the library's Web site requires familiarity with both HTML and form scripts. (For further information and templates for HTML forms see Figures 9-4 and 9-5.) If staff members are not familiar with these,

(continued on p. 173)

Figure 9-1: Bookstrap Template

Patron Name:

Request ID:

Due Date:

Please Return to Interlibrary Loan!

Special Conditions:
- ☐ Library Use Only
- ☐ No Renewal
- ☐ No Photocopying

Contact the ILL office before the due date if you need to renew this item.

Please do not remove this strap.

Your Library
123 Main Street
Anytown, NY 10011
212–123–4567
illborrowing@yourinstitution.com

Patron Name:

Request ID:

Due Date:

Please Return to Interlibrary Loan!

Special Conditions:
- ☐ Library Use Only
- ☐ No Renewal
- ☐ No Photocopying

Contact the ILL office before the due date if you need to renew this item.

Please do not remove this strap.

Your Library
123 Main Street
Anytown, NY 10011
212–123–4567
illborrowing@yourinstitution.com

Figure 9-2: Book Label

Patron Name: Request ID:

Due Date:

Please return to Interlibrary Loan!
Special Conditions:
- ☐ Library Use Only
- ☐ No Renewal
- ☐ No Photocopying

Contact the ILL office before the due date if you need to renew this item.Please do not remove this strap.

Your Library
123 Main Street
Anytown, NY 10011
212–123–4567
illborrowing@yourInstitution.com

Patron Name: Request ID:

Due Date:

Please return to Interlibrary Loan!
Special Conditions:
- ☐ Library Use Only
- ☐ No Renewal
- ☐ No Photocopying

Contact the ILL office before the due date if you need to renew this item. Please do not remove this strap.

Your Library
123 Main Street
Anytown, NY 10011
212–123–4567
illborrowing@yourinstitution.com

Patron Name: Request ID:

Due Date:

Please return to Interlibrary Loan!
Special Conditions:
- ☐ Library Use Only
- ☐ No Renewal
- ☐ No Photocopying

Contact the ILL office before the due date if you need to renew this item. Please do not remove this strap.

Your Library
123 Main Street
Anytown, NY 10011
212–123–4567
illborrowing@yourinstitution.com

Patron Name: Request ID:

Due Date:

Please return to Interlibrary Loan!
Special Conditions:
- ☐ Library Use Only
- ☐ No Renewal
- ☐ No Photocopying

Contact the ILL office before the due date if you need to renew this item. Please do not remove this strap.

Your Library
123 Main Street
Anytown, NY 10011
212–123–4567
illborrowing@yourinstitution.com

Patron Name: Request ID:

Due Date:

Please return to Interlibrary Loan!
Special Conditions:
- ☐ Library Use Only
- ☐ No Renewal
- ☐ No Photocopying

Contact the ILL office before the due date if you need to renew this item. Pleasedo not remove this strap.

Your Library
123 Main Street
Anytown, NY 10011
212–123–4567
illborrowing@yourinstitution.com

Patron Name: Request ID:

Due Date:

Please return to Interlibrary Loan!
Special Conditions:
- ☐ Library Use Only
- ☐ No Renewal
- ☐ No Photocopying

Contact the ILL office before the due date if you need to renew this item. Please do not remove this strap.

Your Library
123 Main Street
Anytown, NY 10011
212–123–4567
illborrowing@yourinstitution.com

Figure 9-3: Patron Notification E-mail Templates

Returnable Materials

The item you requested, <title>, is available for pickup at the circulation desk. It is due on <date>.

Any special conditions are indicated on the book [strap or label].

If you have any questions please contact interlibrary loan at illborrowing@yourinstitution.com or <phone number>.

Articles

E-mail Attachment

The article you requested is attached to this e-mail.

If you have any questions please contact interlibrary loan at illborrowing@yourinstitution.com or <phone number>.

Copy

The article you requested is available for pickup at the circulation desk. The copy is yours to keep.

If you have any questions please contact interlibrary loan at illborrowing@yourinstitution.com or <phone number>.

Overdue Materials

The following interlibrary loan material is now overdue. Please return it to the circulation desk.

> <title>
> <author>
> <publisher>
> <year>

There is a fee of $5 per day for overdue interlibrary loan items. Please note that your library privileges are suspended until the item is returned.

If you have any questions please contact interlibrary loan at illborrowing@yourinstitution.com or <phone number>.

Note: These templates can be used to notify patrons when materials arrive. These should be customized for institutional use. Note that it is not necessary to include extensive information for regular requests.

Figure 9-4: HTML Book Request Form

Book Request

This is a generic form for book requests. Note that this form requires some sort of script for processing. There are many lightweight form-processing scripts online. Requiring certain fields, known as validation, also requires additional code. The author created the javascript within the "head" using Mind Palette (http://mindpalette.com/tutorials/validate/index.php), one of the many javascript generators available online.

*–Required Field

Author: _____

Title:* _____

Publisher: _____

Date of Publication: _____

Series: _____

Edition: _____

ISBN: _____

Source (Where did you find this item?): _____

Patron Information

Last Name: _____

First Name: _____

E-mail: _____

Phone Number: _____

How much are you willing to pay for this item? _____

[Submit]

(continued)

(continued)

HTML script:

```
<?xml version="1.0"?>
<!DOCTYPE html PUBLIC "-//W3C//DTD XHTML 1.0
Transitional//EN"
"http://www.w3.org/TR/xhtml1/DTD/xhtml1-
transitional.dtd">
<html xmlns="http://www.w3.org/1999/xhtml">
<head>
  <title>Borrowing Request Form</title>

<script type="text/javascript"><!—
function validateForm() {
with (document.bookrequest) {
var alertMsg = "The following REQUIRED fields\nhave been
left empty:\n";
if (title.value == "") alertMsg += "\nPlease enter a
title!";
if (email.value == "") alertMsg += "\nPlease enter an
email address!";
if (alertMsg != "The following REQUIRED fields\nhave
been left empty:\n") {
alert(alertMsg);
return false;
} else {
return true;
} } }
// —></script>

</head>

<body>
<h1>Book Request</h1>
```

This is a generic form for book requests. Note that this form requires some sort of script for processing. There are many lightweight form processing scripts online.
```
<br /><br />
```
Requiring certain feilds, known as validation, also requires additional code.   The author created the javascript with in the "head" using Mind Palette (http://mindpalette.com/tutorials/validate/index.php), one of the many javascript generators available online.
```
<br /><br />
<form name="bookrequest" form ac-
tion="http://yourinstitution.com/formscript"
```

(continued)

(continued)

```
method="post" onsubmit="return validateForm()">
*=Required Field<br /><br />
Author: <input type="Text" name="author" maxlength="120"
size="75" /> <br /> <br />
Title:* <input type="Text" name="title" maxlength="120"
size="75" /> <br /> <br />
Publisher: <input type="Text" name="publisher"
maxlength="50" size="50" /> <br /> <br />
Date of Publication: <input type="text" name="place"
maxlength="30" size="20" /> <br /> <br />
Series: <input type="Text" name="series" maxlength="100"
size="50" /> <br />
<br />
Edition: <input type="Text" name="edition"
maxlength="15" size="15" /> <br />
<br />
ISBN: <input type="Text" name="isbn" maxlength="13"
size="13" /> <br /><br />
Source (Where did you find this item?): <input
type="Text" name="source" maxlength="10" size="10" />

<h2>Patron Information</h2>

Last Name:<input type="Text" name="lastname"
maxlength="20" size="10" /><br /><br />
First Name: <input type="Text" name="firstname"
maxlength="20" size="10" />
<br /><br />
E-mail: <input type="Text" name="email" maxlength="50"
size="30" /> <br /><br />
Phone Number: <input type="Text" name="phone"
maxlength="13" size="13" /><br /><br />
How much are you willing to pay for this item?
<input type="Text" name="maxcost" maxlength="5" size="5"
/><br /><br />
<input type="Submit" name="Submit Request"
value="Submit" />

</form>

</body>
</html>
```

Figure 9-5: HTML Article Request Form

Article Request

This is a generic form for article requests. It includes more required fields than the book request form. Note that this form requires some sort of script for processing. There are many lightweight form processing scripts online. Requiring certain fields, known as validation, also requires additional code. The author created the javascript within the "head" using Mind Palette (http://mindpalette.com/tutorials/validate/index.php), one of the many javascript generators available online.

*=Required Field

Article Author:

Article Title:*

Journal Title:*

Volume:*

Issue Number:

Year:

Pages (Inclusive):

ISSN/ISBN:

Source (Where did you find this item?):

Patron Information

Last Name:

First Name:

E-mail:

Phone Number:

How much are you willing to pay for this item?

Submit

(continued)

(continued)

HTML script:

```
<?xml version="1.0"?>
<!DOCTYPE html PUBLIC "-//W3C//DTD XHTML 1.0
Transitional//EN"
"http://www.w3.org/TR/xhtml1/DTD/xhtml1-
transitional.dtd">
<html xmlns="http://www.w3.org/1999/xhtml">
<head>
   <title>Borrowing Request Form</title>

<script type="text/javascript"><!-
function validateForm() {
with (document.articlerequest) {
var alertMsg = "The following REQUIRED fields\nhave been
left empty:\n";
if (articletitle.value == "") alertMsg += "\nPlease
enter an article title!";
if (journaltitle.value == "") alertMsg += "\nPlease
enter a journal title!";
if (volume.value == "") alertMsg += "\nPlease enter the
journal volume!";
if (email.value == "") alertMsg += "\nPlease enter your
e-mail address!";
if (alertMsg != "The following REQUIRED fields\nhave
been left empty:\n") {
alert(alertMsg);
return false;
} else {
return true;
} } }

// -></script>

</head>

<body>
<h1>Article Request</h1>

This is a generic form for article requests.  It
includes more required fields than the book request
form. Note that this form requires some sort of script
for processing.  There are many lightweight form
processing scripts online.
<br /><br />
Requiring certain feilds, known as validation, also
requires additional code.   The author created the
javascript with in the "head" using Mind Palette
```

(continued)

(continued)

```
http://mindpalette.com/tutorials/validate/index.php),
one of the many javascript generators available online.
<br /><br />
<form name="article" form
action="http://yourinstitution.com/formscript"
method="post" onsubmit="return validateForm()">
*=Required Field<br /><br />

Article Author: <input type="Text" name="author"
maxlength="120" size="75" /> <br /> <br />
Article Title:* <input type="Text" name="article"
maxlength="120" size="75" /> <br /> <br />
Journal Title:* <input type="Text" name="journal"
maxlength="75" size="75" /> <br /> <br />
Volume:* <input type="text" name="volume" maxlength="5"
size="5" /> <br /> <br />
Issue Number: <input type="Text" name="issue"
maxlength="5" size="5" /> <br /><br />
Year:<input type="Text" name="year" maxlength="4"
size="4" /> <br /><br />
Pages (Inclusive): <input type="Text" name="pages"
maxlength="10" size="5" /> <br /><br />
ISSN/ISBN: <input type="Text" name="issn" maxlength="13"
size="13" /> <br /><br />
Source (Where did you find this item?): <input
type="Text" name="source" maxlength="10" size="10" />

<h2>Patron Information</h2>

Last Name:<input type="Text" name="lastname"
maxlength="20" size="10" /><br /><br />
First Name: <input type="Text" name="firstname"
maxlength="20" size="10" />
<br /><br />
E-mail: <input type="Text" name="email" maxlength="50"
size="30" /> <br /><br />
Phone Number: <input type="Text" name="phone"
maxlength="13" size="13" /><br /><br />
How much are you willing to pay for this item?
<input type="Text" name="maxcost" maxlength="5" size="5"
/><br /><br />
<input type="Submit" name="Submit Request"
value="Submit" />

</form>

</body>
</html>
```

forms can also be created in word-processing software. If this method is used, staff members should use tables within the document to create the needed fields. Although they are not as common, forms can also be created using spreadsheet software. Spreadsheet forms are easier to fill out because the width of fields can be appropriately sized and locked. Both of these methods eliminate the dreaded and ubiquitous underline open field formatting that is often found in forms created in word processing software.

Once all of the templates and forms are created, the department is ready to begin implementing paperless office procedures. In order to simplify operations, two e-mail addresses should be set up for the department: illborrowing@yourinstitution.com and illlending@yourinstitution.com. The library's Web site should include a page dedicated to interlibrary loan and document delivery. This page should include the patron policy, the lending policy, and links to both borrowing and lending forms.

Borrowing Procedures for the Paperless ILL Office

As patrons usually conduct research using the library's OPAC and databases, borrowing request forms should be accessible on the library's Web site. If possible, the library's OPAC should include a direct link to the online forms. Small departments can determine whether they wish to use one form for both loan and photocopy requests or have a separate form for each.

Some departments might prefer to use the ALA ILL form in PDF writable format that is freely available in the ALA Web site. However, this form includes a lot of extraneous fields for internal use that might confuse the patron. Instead of using the ALA form for patrons, small departments should consider developing local forms for borrowing.

Receiving Requests

Locally developed borrowing request forms, whether in HTML or word-processing format, will not automatically populate with information from the OPAC or other search instruments the patron might use. He or she will have to print or write down citation information and enter it into the form manually. As the forms are online, patrons can use the cut and paste function to complete the fields. Using this method should reduce transcription errors. The HTML form scripts should be set to e-mail completed forms to illborrowing@yourinstitution.com. Forms in other formats should include explicit directions for e-mailing the document to the department. Depending on the patron population, ILL department staff may want to consider giving directions for sending the information within the body of an e-mail rather than as an attachment. In either case, all e-mails addressed to illborrowing@yourinstitution.com should be filtered to a separate inbox folder, preferably one that is accessible to all members of the department.

Finding Materials

In the past few years, it has become much easier to find library holdings information online. OCLC's Open WorldCat (worldcat .org) should be staff members' first place to search for supplying libraries. Open WorldCat allows users to set up personalized accounts for the Web site. As mentioned in Chapter 6, small departments should use one account for the entire department and add cooperating network libraries to the "Favorite Libraries" list.

Once items are found, the search results on WorldCat include a link that leads directly to the holding library's Web site. Many of these will include interlibrary loan information for borrowing libraries. In order to maintain paperless operations, borrowing libraries should send completed ALA ILL request forms by e-mail. If the borrowing library does not accept requests via e-mail, staff members should send the form via fax.

Receiving Materials

In the paperless interlibrary loan office, as much material as possible should be received electronically. Small departments are encouraged to set up Atlas Systems, Inc.'s free Odyssey software on the department computer. This will allow the staff members to send and receive documents to any other library that uses the Odyssey protocol including those that use OCLC's ILLiad IMS. Many libraries do not use the protocol, therefore request forms should indicate that the department can also receive documents via e-mail (the preferred method) or fax.

Once items are received, they should be sent to the patron via e-mail as an attachment. Returnable materials should be processed according to the suggestions given in Chapter 7. Note that the only item that might have been printed out at this point is a bookstrap or label for returnable materials or a faxed document. The entire process from request to receipt was entirely paperless.

Tracking Borrowed Items

As with many other ILL functions, there is enormous payoff in thinking about how to track borrowed items systematically. Several aspects of the borrowing process that need to be monitored include tracking borrowed requests from the time they are received until they are closed, keeping track of returnable items, and maintaining records for copyright compliance.

In the paperless office, borrowing requests should be managed electronically. The department should have a shared folder labeled "ILL Borrowing" on a computer that is backed up regularly. This folder should have several subfolders labeled Pending, Received, and Completed. The electronic request forms are moved from one subfolder to another depending on stage of the request.

Once a request is received via e-mail, the "Save As" function allows the information in the e-mail to be saved in any format. It is easiest (and uses less disk space) to save the electronic requests as a text file (.txt). All of the files should be renamed using the patron's last name as the first part of the title. For example, a request from Paul Smith would be named "Smith 11-1-08." If there are multiple requests from the same person, a numerical identifier should be added to the file name: "4 Smith 11-1-08," "5 Smith 11-1-08," etc. If there is more than one "Smith," the patron's first initial should be added after the last name. Using these conventions consistently allows staff members to take advantage of the file sorting function (Right click, hover on Sort by, then click on Name). The self-made paperless interlibrary loan department does not use computer assigned tracking numbers within the request; therefore, it makes sense to keep track of requests by patron name.

Once requested items arrive, the "Pending" folder files should be sorted in order to easily find the patron's name. All of the information needed for notifying the patron can be found in the saved form. After preparing the item for the patron, the request file should be cut and pasted to the "Received" folder if the item is returnable or the "Completed folder" if the requested item is a photocopy.

To maintain patron privacy, staff members should erase identifying information within the request once files are moved to the completed folder. If for some reason, such as billing procedures or documentation, the patron's name must remain on the request. Staff members should keep identifying information on the request until all procedures are complete. The files should also be renamed using the date of completion. If there is more than one request for a certain date, these files should be numbered sequentially.

The most difficult aspect of this entire system is remembering to "physically" move the files from one folder to another. However, it is important to remember that this "physical" movement keeps track of the status of requests without having to print them and then file them away in hard-copy.

As discussed in Chapter 7, small departments can use several options to keep track of returnable items. One of the easiest is to create a flat file database in spreadsheet software (see Figure 9-6).

Figure 9-6: Borrowed Item Due Dates			
Last Name	**First Name**	**Title**	**Due Date**
Smith	John	Interlibrary Loan	2/29/09
Smith	John	Of All times...	3/12/09
Williams	Jenny	From roots to Fruits	3/19/09
Brown	Peter	Die Kirche	3/21/09
Lee	David	33 Things to Do	4/4/09
Brown	Elizabeth	Making Life Better	4/15/09
Williams	Jenny	Holidays Together	4/20/09
Gordon	Michael	Parts and Hikes	5/1/09
Day	Laurie	Italian Cookbook	5/3/09
Harper	Joyce	Easy Cleaning	5/28/09

This file should also be kept in the "ILL Borrowing" folder on the departmental computer that is regularly backed up. The chart should have four fields: last name of the patron, first name of the patron, title of the item, and the due date. If the department wishes to do so, another field for request ID can be added as spreadsheet software can automatically generate and assign sequential numbers to each row. When returnable materials are received, the information for each item should be entered into the chart. The sort function can be used to keep the nearest due date at the top of the chart no matter when an item is received. Patrons should be sent a reminder e-mail one week before the item is due.

Copyright for article requests can also be tracked using a flat file spreadsheet database (see Figure 9-7). This spreadsheet should have four fields: date received, article title, journal title, journal date/volume/number. Each time an article is received, the information should be entered into the spreadsheet. Note that staff members must be familiar with how to sort using several fields for this tracking method to work. After entering the information, the fields should be sorted according to journal title, article title, and then date received. All staff members who work on interlibrary

Figure 9-7: Copyright Compliance Chart

Date Received	Article Title	Journal Title	Journal Date/ Vol/No
1/21/2009	E-Books Today	Library Automation	Spring 2009 4/1
2/12/2009	Web 2.0	New York Library	December 2006
4/15/2009	The New OPAC	Library Automation	Fall 2008 3/3
4/20/2009	Neutral Questions	Reference Today	May 2007
5/15/2009	EEthnography and Reference Services	Library Science	Summer 2005 53/1
6/4/2009	Censorship in Public Libraries	Library Science	Fall 2006 54/2
6/22/2009	Document Delivery	ILL Today	January 2007
6/29/2009	Streamline Billing	ILL Today	January 2007
7/8/2009	Copyright and Libraries	Library Science	Summer 2005 53/1
7/16/2009	Better Interfaces	Library Automation	Fall 2009 4/3

loan should be alerted via e-mail if there is a title that has four requests. This will ensure that they will be on the lookout for another request of the title.

The interlibrary loan department should also maintain transaction statistics. Another spreadsheet chart should be used for this purpose (see Figure 9-8). As mentioned in Chapter 5, these statistics should be used to determine the department's fill rate for evaluation purposes. The fill rate is the number of requests filled divided by the number of requests received multiplied by 100.

Lending Procedures for the Paperless ILL Office

The home-grown paperless ILL office should encourage requesting libraries to send electronic lending requests whenever possi-

Figure 9-8: ILL Statistics Chart

Week	Lending Requests	Items Lent		Borrowing Requests	Items Received	
		Books	Photo-copies		Books	Photo-copies
2/1/2009	9	3	0	0	1	0
2/8/2009	3	2	1	12	5	0
2/15/2009	13	7	2	2	4	0
2/22/2009	8	3	0	0	4	0
3/1/2009	10	7	0	0	1	0
3/8/2009	9	5	0	0	0	0
3/15/2009	0	0	0	0	0	0
3/22/2009	1	0	0	3	1	0
3/29/2009	12	6	1	1	0	0
4/5/2009	4	3	0	0	2	0
4/12/2009	9	5	0	0	0	0
4/19/2009	10	7	1	3	0	0
4/26/2009	10	2	1	1	0	1
5/3/2009	12	9	0	1	1	0
5/10/2009	6	3	0	0	0	1
5/17/2009	9	4	1	0	2	0
5/24/2009	7	3	1	2	0	0
5/31/2009	9	5	2	0	0	0
6/7/2009	18	12	0	1	2	1
6/14/2009	6	4	0	2	0	0
6/21/2009	2	1	0	2	3	0
6/28/2009	9	7	0	2	0	2
7/5/2009	8	2	3	1	0	0
7/12/2009	8	5	1	0	1	0
Totals	192	105	14	33	27	5

Lending Fill Rate – 62%   Borrowing Fill Rate – 97%

ble. This can be accomplished through several methods. Along with the patron request form, the library's ILL Web page should also include a link to a lending form. Instead of creating their own form for borrowing requests, small departments are encouraged to provide a link to the writable PDF version of the ALA ILL form. Even though the writable PDF is not the easiest electronic file to use, staff members at the requesting library should be familiar with all of the elements that are included on it. If staff members are feeling ambitious, an HTML lending request form similar to the borrowing form can also be created and posted to the library's Web site.

Receiving Requests

Lending information on the Web page should include explicit but simple directions regarding how to send the request. The ALA PDF form must be downloaded and saved to a computer at the requesting library. It should then be sent as an attachment to illlending@yourinstitution.com. If the small department chooses to create a local HTML form, this should also be sent to this e-mail address. As with borrowing, all of lending requests should be automatically filtered to an e-mail inbox folder labeled "ILL Lending."

Finding and Processing Materials

Even though it is tempting to do so, it is not necessary to print these requests. Requests for lending should be reviewed online whenever possible. Staff members should write down call numbers and other identifying information on a separate piece of paper. Requests for returnable materials should only be printed after the item is found on the shelf. Responses to requests that cannot be filled should be sent via e-mail. If the department uses a locally made form instead of the ALA form, staff members should have an e-mail template that includes all of the "Reasons for No" that is saved in a shared ILL folder. Staff members can simply mark the template appropriately and send the response to the requesting institution.

Atlas System's Odyssey should be used for document delivery if the department has set up the software and the requesting institution can receive materials using the Odyssey protocol. Otherwise, staff members should use the all-in-one to scan materials into PDF format. The resulting file can be saved to either the shared drive or the attached hard drive.

If the request was sent using the PDF ILL form, this should be filled out and sent as an attachment along with the requested item. Or, if staff members are able to do so, the request can be inserted into the scanned PDF file. Requests from the library's online form should be copied and pasted into the body of the e-mail with only the requested file attached. Returnable materials should be processed following established procedures.

Tracking Returnable Materials

In a paperless ILL office, returnable materials can be tracked using two methods. If the department uses the suggestion from Chapter 7 of checking out materials to a dummy ILL patron with a long charge period, the library's ILS will send notifications to the appropriate staff member when material is overdue. These notices can be forwarded to the requesting library. Note that this method would only alert libraries when items are very overdue.

The second method involves setting up a spreadsheet similar to the one used to track borrowed items (see Figure 9-9). It should be used if departments wish to notify libraries more quickly about overdue books. This chart would include the following fields: due date, title, and borrowing library. When materials are checked out to the ILL patron, identifying information for the item should be entered into the chart. Note that the actual due date for the book (four weeks or whatever the date policy dictates) rather than the

Figure 9-9: Loaned Item Due Dates			
ILL Number	**Library**	**Title**	**Due Date**
100001	Big Library	Solve It!	3/4/2008
110031	Small Library	Interlibrary Loan	4/15/2008
123456	City College	US History	4/20/2008
222222	State University	Culture	5/1/2008
238910	Big Library	From Roots to Fruits	7/3/2008
259816	Big Library	33 Things to Do	7/18/2008
357892	City College	Making Life Better	7/30/2008
453109	State University	Holidays Together	8/29/2008
463982	Small College	Parks and Hikes	9/5/2008
508901	City College	Italian Cookbook	9/17/2008

ILS due date (two to four months) should be indicated in the chart. This spreadsheet should be sorted by due date and checked on a regular basis. Once items are overdue, staff members can send a notice to the borrowing library using a previously developed template.

Systematic Handling of Payments and Accounts

Keeping track of fee payments is an area of the paper office that must be handled systematically. Several issues must be addressed by any fee accounting system. First, how will the department receive payments? Second, how are patrons and institutions informed of what they owe? Finally, how are these transactions monitored? Small departments without access to an interlibrary loan fee management (IFM) system or other billing system should use a combination of office productivity software and low-cost commercially available payment Web sites to collect and account for ILL fees.

First, small interlibrary loan departments should consider how payments for fees will be accepted. The paperless office does not demand any particular payment method and small departments should develop a system that works best for the institutional situation. However, as long as so much of the process is transferred online, small departments might want to consider collecting fees online as well. Third-party payment processing sites such as PayPal are easily integrated into the library's Web site. Payment processing site accounts can be used to collect not only ILL fees but other patron fees for overdue or lost materials. The entire library might want to consider implementing online payment options to give patrons more payment options for any fees they might incur.

These systems do cost money to use and generally charge a small processing fee for each transaction. However, the convenience of collecting payments online often outweighs the cost of using the service. Online processing Web sites sometimes offer discounts for nonprofit institutions. These sites have several options for payment other than using a credit card, including direct bank withdrawals. Patrons are not required to have an account with the Web site or a credit card to use the payment services.

There are several Web site integration methods libraries can use depending on the information technology support that is available in the institution. For example, PayPal offers options ranging from a simple button that is placed on a Web page to fully customizable coding options for Web site developers. Library staff members must decide which option works best for their institution

The second issue that must be addressed concerning payments involves deciding how to inform patrons and institutions of any fees they might owe. Locally made HTML forms should indicate the fees for lending and borrowing. If the department uses the templates in this chapter, patrons must add up and enter the fee total themselves as the forms' fields do not automatically populate. In order to facilitate this process, the fees should be easy to calculate. For example, rather than charging a per page fee for photocopies, homegrown paperless ILL departments should charge a per transaction fee for both photocopies and returnable materials.

Lending fees should be fully described on the library's interlibrary loan Web page. As this information cannot be added to the ALA ILL form, lending requests need to be carefully matched with payments that are received online. Invoices for borrowing request fees can be created easily in word processing software. These should be sent via e-mail to the requesting library.

Spreadsheets can also be used to monitor interlibrary loan fees. This chart should include the following fields: invoice number, date sent, borrowing institution, fee amount, date received, and amount received. It should also include a field for request identification such as a locally generated number or the title of the requested item. This chart should be updated whenever fees are assessed.

Streamlining the Paperless ILL and Document Delivery Office

As long as staff members follow the "think before you print" maxim, creating a paperless ILL office is not difficult. One issue that many people encounter when creating their own electronic filing system is the need to replicate information in many different places. None of the suggested procedures requires all of the fields in either the borrowing or lending forms to be entered into the tracking spreadsheets.

Even though the procedures here describe an idealized situation, any of the suggestions can be used to streamline workflows in small interlibrary loan departments. Creating a low-cost paperless ILL office requires a fair amount of preparatory work. However, with a bit of effort, any ILL department can go paperless without using the systems described in the previous chapter.

Appendix A

Interlibrary Loan Code
for the United States

Prepared by RUSA's Interlibrary Loan Committee, 1994, revised
2001. Revised 2008, by the Sharing and Transforming Access to
Resources Section (STARS). Approved by the RUSA Board of
Directors, 2009.

Introduction

The Reference and User Services Association, acting for the
American Library Association in its adoption of this code, recognizes that the sharing of material between libraries is an integral
element in the provision of library service and believes it to be in
the public interest to encourage such an exchange.

In the interest of providing quality service, libraries have an obligation to obtain material to meet the informational needs of users
when local resources do not meet those needs. Interlibrary loan
(ILL), a mechanism for obtaining material, is essential to the vitality of all libraries.

The effectiveness of the national interlibrary loan system depends upon participation of libraries of all types and sizes.

This code establishes principles that facilitate the requesting of
material by a library and the provision of loans or copies in response to those requests. In this code, "material" includes books,
audiovisual materials, and other returnable items as well as copies

of journal articles, book chapters, excerpts, and other non-returnable items.

1.0 Definition

1.1   Interlibrary loan is the process by which a library requests material from, or supplies material to, another library.

2.0 Purpose

2.1   The purpose of interlibrary loan as defined by this code is to obtain, upon request of a library user, material not available in the user's local library.

3.0 Scope

3.1   This code regulates the exchange of material between libraries in the United States.

3.2   Interlibrary loan transactions with libraries outside of the United States are governed by the International Federation of Library Associations and Institutions' International Lending: Principles and Guidelines for Procedure.

4.0 Responsibilities of the Requesting Library

4.1   Establish, promptly update, and make available an interlibrary borrowing policy.

4.2   Ensure the confidentiality of the user.

4.3   Describe completely and accurately the requested material following accepted bibliographic practice.

4.4   Identify libraries that own the requested material and check and adhere to the policies of potential supplying libraries.

4.5   When no libraries can be identified as owning the needed material, requests may be sent to libraries believed likely to own the material, accompanied by an indication that ownership is not confirmed.

4.6   Transmit interlibrary loan requests electronically whenever possible.

4.7   For copy requests, comply with the U.S. copyright law (Title 17, U.S. Code) and its accompanying guidelines.

4.8   Assume responsibility for borrowed material from the time it leaves the supplying library until it has been returned to and received by the supplying library. This includes all material shipped directly to and/or returned by the user. If damage or loss occurs, provide compensation or replacement, in accordance with the preference of the supplying library.

4.9   Assume full responsibility for user-initiated transactions.

4.10   Honor the due date and enforce any use restrictions specified by the supplying library. The due date is defined as the date the material is due to be checked-in at the supplying library.

4.11   Request a renewal before the item is due. If the supplying library does not respond, the requesting library may assume that a renewal has been granted extending the due date by the same length of time as the original loan.

4.12   All borrowed material is subject to recall. Respond immediately if the supplying library recalls an item.

4.13   Package material to prevent damage in shipping and comply with any special instructions stated by the supplying library.

4.14   Failure to comply with the provisions of this code may be reason for suspension of service by a supplying library.

5.0 Responsibilities of the Supplying Library

5.1   Establish, promptly update, and make available an interlibrary lending policy.

5.2   Consider filling all requests for material regardless of format.

5.3   Ensure the confidentiality of the user.

5.4   Process requests in a timely manner that recognizes the needs of the requesting library and/or the requirements of the electronic network or transmission system being used. If unable to fill a request, respond promptly and should state the reason the request cannot be filled.

5.5   When filling requests, send sufficient information with each item to identify the request.

5.6   Indicate the due date and any restrictions on the use of the material and any special return packaging or shipping requirements. The due date is defined as the date the material is due to be checked-in at the supplying library.

5.7   Ship material in a timely and efficient manner to the location specified by the requesting library. Package loaned material to prevent loss or damage in shipping. Deliver copies electronically whenever possible.

5.8   Respond promptly to requests for renewals. If no response is sent, the requesting library may assume that a renewal has been granted extending the due date by the same length of time as the original loan.

5.9   Loaned material is subject to recall material at any time.

5.10   Failure to comply with the provisions of this code may lead to suspension of service to the requesting library.

ILL Code for the United States Explanatory Supplement

For Use with the Interlibrary Loan Code for the United States (May 2008)

This Explanatory Statement is intended to amplify specific sections of the Interlibrary Loan Code for the United States, providing fuller explanation and specific examples for text that is intentionally general and prescriptive. Topical headings in these Guidelines refer to the equivalent sections in the Code. Libraries are expected to comply with the Code, using this Supplement as a source for general direction.[1]

Introduction

The U.S. Interlibrary Loan Code, first published in 1917 and adopted by The American Library Association in 1919, is designed to provide a code of behavior for requesting and supplying material within the United States. This code does not override individual or consortial agreements or regional or state codes which may be more liberal or more prescriptive. This national code is intended to provide guidelines for exchanges between libraries where no other agreement applies. The code is intended to be adopted voluntarily by U.S. libraries and is not enforced by an oversight body. However, as indicated below, supplying libraries may suspend service to borrowing libraries that fail to comply with the provisions of this code.

This interlibrary loan code describes the responsibilities of libraries to each other when requesting material for users. Increasingly libraries are allowing users to request material directly from suppliers. This code makes provision for direct patron requesting and at the same time affirms the responsibility of the patron's library for the safety and return of the borrowed material, or for paying the cost of a non-returnable item sent directly to the patron.

Technology has expanded access options beyond traditional library-to-library transactions. Unmediated requests, direct-to-user delivery, purchase-on-demand options, and increasing full-text availability are exciting developments in resource sharing. At present, the Interlibrary Loan Code reflects established practices. However, libraries and other information centers are encouraged to explore and use non-traditional means where available to ensure maximum accessibility and convenience for users. More information for libraries interested in new ideas for resource sharing can be found at:

http://www.ala.org/ala/rusa/rusaourassoc/rusasections/stars/ starssections/committeesa/rrscomm/rrscomm.cfm.

1. Definition

The Interlibrary Code for the United States covers transactions between two libraries. Transactions between libraries and commercial document suppliers or library fee-based services are contractual arrangements beyond the scope of these guidelines.

The terms "requesting library" and "supplying library" are used in preference to "borrowing" and "lending" to cover the exchange of copies as well as loans.

2. Purpose

Interlibrary loan (ILL) is intended to complement local collections and is not a substitute for good library collections intended to meet the routine needs of users. ILL is based on a tradition of sharing resources between various types and sizes of library and rests on the belief that no library, no matter how large or well supported, is self-sufficient in today's world. It is also evident that some libraries are net borrowers (borrow more than they lend) and others are net lenders (lend more than they borrow), but the system of interlibrary loan still rests on the belief that all libraries should be willing to lend if they are willing to borrow.

3. Scope

The conduct of international interlibrary loan is regulated by the rules set forth in the IFLA document International Lending: Principles and Guidelines for Procedure.[2]

Although the U.S. shares a common border with Canada and Mexico, it is important to remember that these countries have their own library infrastructures and ILL codes. The IFLA Principles and Guidelines regulate the exchange of material between institutions across these borders. Further, U.S. librarians would be wise to inform themselves of customs requirements that take precedence over library agreements when material is shipped across these national borders, e.g., as described in the Association of Research Libraries' Transborder Interlibrary Loan: Shipping Interlibrary Loan Materials from the U.S. to Canada.[3]

4. Responsibilities of the Requesting Library

4.1 Written Policies

A library's interlibrary loan borrowing policy should be available in a written format that is readily accessible to all library users.

Whenever possible the borrowing policy should be posted on the library's Web site as well as be available in paper copy at public service desks or wherever other library user handouts are provided.

4.2 Confidentiality

Interlibrary loan transactions, like circulation transactions, are confidential library records. Interlibrary loan personnel are encouraged to be aware of local/state confidentiality rules and laws as they relate to interlibrary loan transactions. Appropriate steps, such as using identification numbers or codes rather than users' names, should be taken to maintain confidentiality. However, it is not a violation of this code to include a user's name on a request submitted to a supplier. Policies and procedures should be developed regarding the retention of ILL records and access to this information. ILL personnel should also be aware of privacy issues when posting requests for assistance or using the text of ILL requests as procedural examples. ALA's Office for Intellectual Freedom has developed a number of policies regarding confidentiality of library records.[4]

ILL staff should adhere to the American Library Association's (ALA) Code of Ethics,[5] specifically principle III, that states: "We protect each library user's right to privacy and confidentiality with respect to information sought or received and resources consulted, borrowed, acquired or transmitted."

4.3 Complete Bibliographic Citation

A good bibliographic description is the best assurance that the user will receive the item requested. Rather than detail these descriptive elements, the code requires the requesting library to include whatever data provides the best indication of the desired material, whether an alphanumeric string or an extensive bibliographic citation. The important point is that this description be exact enough to avoid unnecessary work on the part of the supplier and frustration on the part of the user. For example, journal title verification rather than article level verification would be sufficient.

4.4 Identifying Appropriate Suppliers

Requesting libraries should use all resources at their disposal to determine ownership of a particular title before sending a request to a potential supplier. Many libraries contribute their holdings to major bibliographic utilities such as DOCLINE and/or OCLC and make their individual catalogs freely available via the Internet. The interlibrary loan listserv (ill-l@webjunction.org) or other ILL-related lists are also excellent sources for the requesting library to verify and/or locate particularly difficult items.

The requesting library is encouraged to use resources such as the OCLC Policies Directory to determine lending policies, including any applicable charges, before requesting material.

The requesting library should clearly state on the request an amount that meets or exceeds the charges of suppliers to which the request is sent. The requesting library is responsible for payment of any fees charged by the supplying library that are less than or equal to the amount stated on its request. Libraries are encouraged to use electronic invoicing capabilities such as OCLC's Interlibrary Loan Fee Management (IFM) system or the Electronic Fund Transfer System used by medical libraries.

4.5 Sending Unverified Requests

Despite the requirements in Sec. 4.4 and 4.5 that an item should be completely and accurately described and located, the code recognizes that it is not always possible to verify and/or locate a particular item. For example, a request may be sent to a potential supplier with strong holdings in a subject or to the institution at which the dissertation was written.

4.6 Transmitting the Request

The code recommends electronic communication. For many libraries, sending requests electronically means using the ILL messaging systems associated with DOCLINE, OCLC, other products that use the ISO ILL Protocol, or structured e-mail requests.

Lacking the ability to transmit in this fashion, the requesting library should send a completed ALA interlibrary loan request form via fax, Internet transmission, or mail; use a potential supplier's Web request form; or otherwise provide the necessary information via e-mail message or conventional letter. Whatever communication method is used, the requesting library should identify and use the appropriate address or number for ILL requests.

The requesting library should include a street address, a postal box number, an IP address, a fax number, and an e-mail address to give the supplying library delivery options. Any special needs, such as for a particular edition, language, or rush delivery, should be included on the request.

In addition, because the primary purpose of interlibrary loan is to provide material for relatively short-term use by an individual, the requesting library should communicate with the supplying library in advance if the material is needed for other uses (such as course reserves, classroom or other group viewing of audio-visual material or for an extended loan period, especially of a textbook).

4.7 Copy Requests

The requesting library is responsible for complying with the provisions of Section 108(g)(2) Copyright Law[6] and the Guidelines for the Proviso of Subsection 108(g)(2) prepared by the National

Commission on New Technological Uses of Copyrighted Works (the CONTU Guidelines).[7]

4.8 Responsibility of the Requester

The requesting library assumes an inherent risk when material is supplied through interlibrary loan. Although the number is small, some material is lost or damaged at some point along the route from the supplier and back again. The requesting library's responsibility for this loss is based on the concept that if the request had not been made, the material would not have left the supplier's shelf, and thus would not have been put at risk. This section clearly states that the requesting library is responsible for the material from the time it leaves the supplying library until its safe return to the supplying library.

If the requesting library asks for delivery at a location away from the library (such as to the user's home), the requesting library is likewise responsible for the material during this delivery and return process. In any case, a final decision regarding replacement, repair, or compensation rests with the supplying library.

Borrowed items should be returned in the condition in which they were received at the requesting library. In particular, adhesive labels or tape should not be affixed directly to any borrowed item.

It is the responsibility of the requesting library to pay invoices received or to notify the supplying library of any billing questions not later than six months from the billing date for the charges in question. The requesting library should also make every attempt to resolve billing questions within six months of notifying the supplying library of an apparent billing error.

Although the code stipulates that the requesting library is required to pay if billed for a lost or damaged item, the supplying library is not necessarily required to charge for a lost item. In the case of lost material, the requesting and supplying libraries may need to work together to resolve the matter. For instance, the library shipping the material may need to initiate a trace with the delivery firm.

4.9 Responsibility for Unmediated ILL Requests

Some requesting libraries permit users to initiate online ILL requests that are sent directly to potential supplying libraries. A requesting library that chooses to allow its users to order materials through interlibrary loan without mediation accepts responsibility for these requests as if they have been placed by library staff. The supplying library may assume that the user has been authenticated and authorized to place requests and that the requesting library assumes full responsibility for transaction charges, the safety and return of material, and the expense of replacement or repair.

4.10 Due Date and Use Restrictions

This code makes a departure from earlier codes that described due dates in terms of a "loan period" which was interpreted as the length of time a requesting library could retain the material before returning it. The primary object of this section is to provide a clear definition of due date as the date the material must be checked in at the supplying library. This definition brings ILL practice into alignment with automated circulation procedures and is intended to facilitate interoperability of ILL and circulation applications.

The requesting library should develop a method for monitoring due dates so that material can be returned to and checked in at the supplying library by the due date assigned by the supplying library.

The requesting library is responsible for ensuring compliance with any use restrictions specified by the supplying library such as "library use only" or "no photocopying."

4.11 Renewals

When the supplying library denies a renewal request the material should be returned by the original due date or as quickly as possible if the renewal is denied after the due date has passed.

4.12 Recalls

The response to a recall may be the immediate return of the material, or timely communication with the supplying library to negotiate a new due date.

When the material has been recalled, the requesting library is encouraged to return the material via an expedited delivery carrier such as UPS, FedEx, or USPS Priority Mail.

4.13 Shipping

It is the ultimate responsibility of the requesting library to return materials in the same condition in which they were received as noted in section 4.8 of the Interlibrary Loan Code for the United States.

It is the responsibility of the requesting library to follow the shipping and packaging requirements, including insurance and preferred shipping method, as stipulated by the supplying library. Packaging is defined as the outer material, which may be a box, padded envelope, etc. Wrapping is defined as an inner covering for the item such as paper or bubble wrap.

If no shipping or packaging methods are specified, the requesting library's regular form of shipment should be used.

If packaging material has been used previously, remove or mark out old addresses, postal marks, etc., to avoid misdirection. Do not reuse old, frayed, ripped, or decaying packaging and wrapping materials—discard it instead. Clearly address all packages with both the destination and return addresses properly attached to the packaging material.

In accordance with United States Postal Service guidelines, tape is the preferred sealing method on all types of packages. Remember that wrapping and packaging materials will most likely be reused. So, please use tape judiciously. If staples must be used, do not use industrial (e.g., copper) staples if at all possible. Copper staples make it very difficult to reuse wrapping and packaging materials and are not ergonomically sound.

Use wrapping and packaging material that is appropriate to the size and format of the material being shipped. Too small or too large packaging will not adequately protect materials during transportation. Remember to use appropriate wrapping to avoid shifting and damage to the contents.

For special formats, consult the appropriate ALA Guidelines:

- American Library Association. Association for Library Collections and Technical Services. Guidelines for Packaging and Shipping Magnetic Tape Recording and Optical Discs (CD-ROM and CD-R) Carrying Audio, Video, and/or Data, n.d.
- American Library Association. Association for Library Collections and Technical Services. Guidelines for Packaging and Shipping Microforms, 1989.
- American Library Association. Association for Library Collections and Technical Services. Guidelines for Preservation Photocopying of Replacement Pages, 1990.
- American Library Association. Video Round Table. Guidelines for the Interlibrary Loan of Audiovisual Formats, 1998.
- American Library Association. Association of College and Research Libraries. Ad Hoc Committee on the Interlibrary Loan of Rate and Unique Materials.Guidelines for the Interlibrary Loan of Rare and Unique Materials, 2004.

4.14 Suspension of Service

Repeated or egregious breaches of this code may result in the requesting library's inability to obtain material. Examples of actions that may result in suspension include lost or damaged books, allowing "library use only" books to leave the library, or failing to pay the supplier's charges. A supplying library should not suspend service to a requesting library without first attempting to resolve the problem(s).

5. Responsibilities of the Supplying Library

5.1 Lending Policy

The lending policy should be clear, detailed, and readily available to requesting libraries. The policy should include among other things, schedule of fees and charges, overdue fines, non-circulating items/categories, current shipping instructions, calendar for service suspensions, penalties for late payments, etc. While a supplying library may charge additional fees for the rapid delivery of requested material, it is recommended that no additional fees be charged for the routine supply of documents via electronic means.

The supplying library is encouraged to make its lending policy available in print, on the library's Web site, and in resources such as the OCLC Policies Directory. The supplying library should be willing to fill requests for all types and classes of users, and all types of libraries, regardless of their size or geographic location.

5.2 Material Format

Supplying libraries are encouraged to lend as liberally as possible regardless of the format of the material requested, while retaining the right to determine what material will be supplied. It is the obligation of the supplying library to consider the loan of material on a case-by-case basis. Supplying libraries are encouraged to lend audiovisual material, newspapers, and other categories of material that have traditionally been non-circulating.

Supplying libraries are encouraged to follow ACRL's Guidelines for the Interlibrary Loan of Rare and Unique Materials[8] and the Guidelines for Interlibrary Loan of Audiovisual Formats.[9]

If permitted by copyright law, the supplying library should consider providing a copy in lieu of a loan rather than giving a negative response.

Supplying libraries should be aware of the provisions of license agreements for electronic resources that may either permit or prohibit use of an electronic resource to fill interlibrary copying requests.

5.3 Confidentiality

The supplying library has a responsibility to safeguard the confidentiality of the individual requesting the material. The sharing of the user's name between requesting and supplying library is not, of itself, a violation of confidentiality. However, the supplying library should not require the user's name if the requesting library chooses not to provide it. If the name is provided, the supplying library needs to take care not to divulge the identity of the person requesting the material.

5.4 Timely Processing

The supplying library has a responsibility to act promptly on all requests. If a supplying library cannot fill a request within a reasonable time then it should respond promptly. The response should be sent via the same method the requesting library used to send the request, or by otherwise contacting the requesting library directly. Some ILL messaging systems such as OCLC and DOCLINE have built-in time periods after which requests will either expire or be sent to another institution. The supplying library should respond before this time expires rather than allow requests to time-out.

Providing a reason for an unfilled request helps the requesting library determine what additional steps, if any, may be taken to access the requested item. For example, "non-circulating" indicates the item is likely available for on-site use while "in use" indicates that another request at a later date might be filled. Providing no reason or simply stating "policy problem" or "other" without providing additional information deprives the requesting library of important information and can lead to time-consuming follow-up for both libraries.

Timely processing of a loan or copy may involve other library departments, such as circulation, copy services, and the mailroom. The interlibrary loan department is responsible for ensuring that material is delivered expeditiously, irrespective of internal library organizational responsibilities.

The supplying library should, when charging for materials, make every effort to allow for a variety of payment options. Payment through electronic crediting and debiting services such as OCLC's ILL Fee Management (IFM) system or other non-invoicing payment forms such as IFLA vouchers should be encouraged. The supplying library that charges should make every effort to accept the use of vouchers, coupons, or credit cards.

It is the responsibility of the supplying library to send final bills for service not later than six months after the supply date, final overdue notices not later than six months after the final due date, and final bills for replacement of lost material not later than one year after the final due date. The supplying library should resolve billing questions within six months of receiving notice of an apparent billing error.

5.5 Identifying the Request

The supplying library should send sufficient identifying information with the material to allow the requesting library to identify the material and process the request quickly. Such information may include a copy of the request, the requestor's transaction number, or the user's ID or name. Failure to include identifying information with the material can unduly delay its processing and may risk the safety of the material.

Supplying libraries are encouraged to enclose an accurate and complete return mailing label.

5.6 Use Restrictions and Due Date

Although it is the responsibility of the requesting library to ensure the safe treatment and return of borrowed material, the supplying library should provide specific instructions when it is lending material that needs special handling. These instructions might include the requirement that material be used only in a monitored special collections area, no photocopying, library use only, specific return packaging/shipping instructions, etc. The supplying library should not send "library use only" material directly to a user.

The supplying library should clearly indicate the date on which it expects the loan to be discharged in its circulation system. As explained in section 4.10 above, this code has moved away from the concept of a loan period, to a definite date that accommodates the sending and return of material as well as sufficient time for the use of the material. For example, a supplying library might establish a due date of six (6) weeks for the purpose of providing one (1) week for shipping, four (4) weeks for use, and one (1) week for the return trip and check-in.

5.7 Delivery and Packaging

The location specified by the requesting library may include the requesting library, a branch or departmental library, or the individual user.

It is the responsibility of the supplying library:

- to judge whether an item is suitable for shipment and circulation. If a damaged item is sent, the supplying library should note all prior damage (such as loose pages or loose spine) and not hold the requesting library responsible for subsequent damage.
- to take care that the material it sends out is properly packaged to protect the item from damage even though the requesting library will be held responsible for material damaged in shipment to specify the shipping method, as well as insurance, for returning materials and if any special wrapping or packaging is required. See section 4.13 above for definitions and other important information regarding wrapping and packaging.
- to provide a complete street address if asking for return via UPS, FedEx, etc. (Many supplying libraries find it safer and more cost effective to ship all material via expedited carriers.)
- to work with the requesting library when tracing a lost or damaged item if the commercial delivery firm is responsible for reimbursement for losses in transit.

5.8 Renewals

The supplying library should respond affirmatively or negatively to all renewal requests. The supplying library is encouraged to grant the renewal request if the material is not needed by a local user.

5.9 Recalls

The supplying library may recall material at its discretion at any time. Increasingly, some libraries are finding it more effective to request the material on ILL for a local user rather than to recall material in use by another library.

5.10 Service Suspension

A supplying library should not suspend service without first attempting to address the problem(s) with the requesting library.

References

1. Boucher, Virginia. *Interlibrary Loan Practices Handbook.* Chicago: American Library Association, 1997. Though written in light of an earlier code, the Practices Handbook contains many useful and practical details on interlibrary loan procedures.

2. International Federation of Library Associations and Institutions. International Lending: Principles and Guidelines for Procedure, 2001.

3. Transborder Interlibrary Loan: Shipping Interlibrary Loan Materials from the U.S. to Canada, 1999. (Note: Pricing information is out of date.)

4. American Library Association. Office for Intellectual Freedom. Policy on Confidentiality of Library Records, 1986. American Library Association. Office for Intellectual Freedom. Policy Concerning Confidentiality of Personally Identifiable Information about Library Users, 2004.

5. American Library Association. Committee on Professional Ethics. Code of Ethics. Chicago: American Library Association, 1995.

6. Copyright Law of the United States of America Chapter 1, Section 108: Limitations on the exclusive rights: Reproduction by libraries and archives.

7. National Commission on New Technological Uses of Copyrighted Works. Guidelines on Photocopying Under Interlibrary Loan Arrangements.

8. American Library Association. Association of College and Research Libraries. Ad Hoc Committee on the Interlibrary Loan

of Rare and Unique Materials. Guidelines for the Loan of Rare and Unique Materials. 2004.

9. American Library Association. Video Round Table. Guidelines for Interlibrary Loan of Audiovisual Formats. 1998.

10. Hilyer, Lee. *Interlibrary Loan and Document Delivery: Best Practices for Operating and Managing Interlibrary Loan Services in All Libraries.* Binghamton, NY: The Haworth Press, 2006. (Co-published simultaneously as *Journal of Interlibrary Loan, Document Delivery & Electronic Reserve,* 16, no. 1/2: 2006.)

11. Hilyer, Lee. *Interlibrary Loan and Document Delivery in the Larger Academic Library: A Guide for University, Research, and Larger Public Libraries.* Binghamton, NY: The Haworth Press, 2002. (Co-published simultaneously as *Journal of Interlibrary Loan, Document Delivery & Information Supply,* 13, no. 1/2: 2002.)

Index

A

Academic Library Borrowing Policy, 112–113
Academic Library Lending Policy, 82
Accessibility, of policies, 70–71, 75–76
Agreements, 30–33
ALA Interlibrary Loan Request Form
  for borrowing libraries, 122
  receiving requests with, 180
  requesting library's use of, 194
  template, 85
  use of, 173
American Library Association (ALA)
  on borrowing materials, 109
  Committee on Professional Ethics, 57–58
  on confidentiality, 130, 192
  definition of ILL, 2–3
  on due dates, 66, 124
  ILL code, adoption of, 14
  ILL history and, 4, 5–7
  Interlibrary Loan Code for the United States, 58–67, 71, 73, 185–188
  Interlibrary Loan Code for the United States Explanatory Supplement, 189–204
  on lending period, 89
  library service outcome studies, 14
  on packaging/shipping, 198
  on participation of libraries, 80
  on responsibility for borrowed material, 122
American Library Journal, 4
American Theological Library Association, 9
Anderson, Joseph, 28–29
Archives, 47
Ariel
  address in policy, 106
  choice of technology, 143
  Clio and, 150
  overview, price, features of, 154–155
  Prospero and, 156
  for receiving photocopies, 125
  sending article via, 96
Association of College and Research Libraries, 7, 14, 87
Association of Research Libraries (ARL)
  copyright protection notice and, 55
  lending to Canada agreement, 83–84
  library service outcome studies, 14
  NAILDD initiative, 11
  U.S./Canada ILL shipping, 60, 191
Atlas Systems
  ILLiad created by, 150–151
  Odyssey, 139, 155, 175
  Odyssey for document delivery, 125, 181
Audio/visual materials, 87
Authors, 42, 44–45

B

Berne Convention Implementation Act of 1988, 44
Berne Convention of 1886, 42–43

207

About the Author

Emily Knox is a doctoral student in the Department of Library and Information Science at the School for Communication and Information at Rutgers University. Her research interests include intellectual freedom and religious censorship. Prior to returning to school, she was the Associate Director and Reference Librarian at the St. Mark's Library of the General Theological Seminary of the Episcopal Church in New York City for five years. Knox received her MSLIS from the University of Illinois Urbana-Champaign in 2003. She currently resides in New Jersey.